My Story

My Story

Create Your Own Digital Family Archive

Adam Juniper

Reader's Digest

The Reader's Digest Association, Inc.
Pleasantville, New York/Montreal/Sydney/Singapore

A READER'S DIGEST BOOK

This edition published by The Reader's Digest Association, Inc.,
by arrangement with Ilex Press Limited

Copyright © 2008 The Ilex Press Limited
This book was conceived, designed, and produced by
The Ilex Press Limited, Cambridge, England.

FOR ILEX PRESS
Publisher: Alastair Campbell
Creative Director: Peter Bridgewater
Managing Editor: Chris Gatcum
Art Director: Julie Weir
Designer: Ginny Zeal
Design Assistant: Emily Harbison

FOR READER'S DIGEST
U.S. Project Editor: Kim Casey
Canadian Project Editor: Pamela Johnson
Australian Project Editor: Annette Carter
Project Designer: George McKeon
Executive Editor, Trade Publishing: Dolores York
Associate Publisher: Rosanne McManus
President and Publisher, Trade Publishing: Harold Clarke

LIBRARY OF CONGRESS CATALOGING-IN-PUBLICATION DATA
Juniper, Adam.
  My story : easy digital tools to archive your life, with photos,
music, videos, and keepsakes / by Adam Juniper.
     p. cm.
  Includes bibliographical references and index.
  ISBN-13: 978-0-7621-0889-3
  ISBN-10: 0-7621-0889-4
  1. Photography—Digital techniques. 2. Scrapbook journaling.
3. Documentary photography. 4. Autobiography. 5. Multimedia
(Art) I. Title.
  TR267.J86 2008
  775—dc22

                               2007049956

We are committed to both the quality of our products
and the service we provide to our customers. We value
your comments, so please feel free to contact us.

          The Reader's Digest Association, Inc.
          Adult Trade Publishing
          Reader's Digest Road
          Pleasantville, NY 10570-7000

For more Reader's Digest products and information,
visit our website:
          www.rd.com (in the United States)
          www.readersdigest.ca (in Canada)
          www.readersdigest.com.au (in Australia)
          www.readersdigest.com.nz (in New Zealand)

Printed in China

1 3 5 7 9 10 8 6 4 2 (Trade)
1 3 5 7 9 10 8 6 4 2 (BAF)

Contents

Introduction

Every one of the six billion people on Earth has a unique story; a single strand in an infinitely complex web of crossing timelines and special moments. One of these is yours, and you are the best person to record the events, people, and places that make your life so distinctive.

Over the years, people have recorded their lives through written diaries. Thanks to these writings, we now have unparalleled insights into some of the most important periods of history through the extraordinary writing of ordinary individuals, such as Anne Frank. Today millions of people keep accounts of their lives in diaries or online through a blog.

A diary, though, consists of words and whatever keepsakes you can tuck in between its pages. When you look back through it, you can't see the moments that matter or hear the music that defined you.

However, in an electronic age when we can take limitless photographs, record hours of High-Definition video, and store an entire music collection in a device the size of a matchbox, there is another way to record your life. This book and the accompanying *My Story* program will help you present your life in its entirety.

Tools of the trade

1

The *My Story* program was created to be as simple as possible, so you can focus on recording your memories and let your computer keep things in order.

This chapter introduces the basic tools you will need, including the minimum requirements for your computer system. It also introduces the *My Story* program, the centerpiece of this book, so you'll have a clear idea of how everything works. This is important, because you don't need to read every chapter before you start.

The rest of the book is divided into chapters that discuss acquiring, adjusting, and improving digital files, as well as detailed instructions on adding them to the *My Story* program. However, before you decide where to go next, you'll need this overview.

Your life story

Computers play a central role in almost all forms of media, including music, video, photography, and communication. They are also extremely valuable and versatile tools that allow us to combine images and sounds in creative ways. Chances are you already have some of your memories in digital form.

The *My Story* program on the CD is designed to help you take these elements—which might be stored in several places in your computer or CD collection—pick out your favorites, and use them to tell the unique story of your life.

This book will not only guide you every step of the way through the *My Story* program, it also devotes a whole chapter to source material to help you turn a meaningful recollection into a digital file—whether it started out as a black-and-white print, or a digital video from your cell phone.

Favorite things
Your story can be made up of anything you want, and you can set up categories for all of your favorite things.

MUSIC	SPORTS	PETS	HISTORY
BOOKS	PEOPLE	MOMENTS	TIME OF YEAR
FILMS	PLACES	FOOD & DRINK	INTERESTS

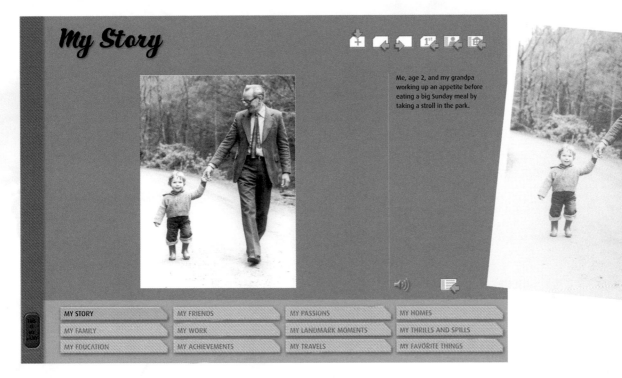

My Story

Me, age 2, and my grandpa working up an appetite before eating a big Sunday meal by taking a stroll in the park.

MY STORY	MY FRIENDS	MY PASSIONS	MY HOMES
MY FAMILY	MY WORK	MY LANDMARK MOMENTS	MY THRILLS AND SPILLS
MY EDUCATION	MY ACHIEVEMENTS	MY TRAVELS	MY FAVORITE THINGS

Print to digital
Black-and-white prints can be scanned into your computer, digitally enhanced, and added into *My Story* when they've been repaired.

Bringing it back to life
Memories can be quickly brought back to life with a few clicks in an image-editing program. You'll find detailed instructions on restoring your memorable photographs beginning on page 114.

Computers

Choosing the perfect computer for your home isn't easy, and if you ask the wrong person it can quickly descend into a bewildering technical discussion. To keep things simple, we've made sure that the *My Story* program is compatible with a broad range of computers. Next you'll become familiar with the basic requirements.

The two most established operating systems for home computers are Apple's Mac OS X and Microsoft Windows. The *My Story* disc will work on both of these systems. Programs that work in one system do not, however, work on the other, so we have supplied a separate version for each system on the same disc. If you insert the disc into a Windows computer, you will only see the Windows version and vice versa.

Apple computers are popular in the home, and the newest ones can also run Microsoft Windows software.

HELP DESK

Upgrading the memory or RAM in your computer will help speed it up—not only when you're using the *My Story* program, but with virtually every other program you have as well.

Depending on the design of your computer, it can be fairly easy to locate a spare memory socket and add a memory module. Even some intricate laptops have easy-to-open covers that reveal the memory slots. Be sure to check the instructions that came with your computer.

MINIMUM REQUIREMENTS

- Your monitor needs a minimum size or resolution of 768 x 1024 pixels to display the *My Story* program correctly.

- You will need a disk drive capable of reading a CD-ROM, which is standard on all modern computers. It may also be a DVD-ROM drive.

- In terms of memory (RAM), your computer will need at least 256 MB, although it will run faster if you have more.

- You will need speakers to hear any sound files or video clips you add. Some older Windows computers can only play sound if an additional sound card is installed. It is very rare that this feature is not included now.

- Your computer needs to be fast enough to play QuickTime movie files. The minimum requirement is a Macintosh G3 (400 MHz processor) or a Pentium-class Windows processor.

Both Mac and Windows systems store information on an internal Hard Disk Drive (HDD). You will need some spare room on your drive to store your story. Once you've copied it from the CD, you can add to *My Story* on your HDD without needing the CD each time you want to expand or modify your story.

A laptop is ideal if you are short on space or need to work away from a power supply.

Quick overview

Whenever you want to edit your story, the *My Story* home page will always be your starting point. It links directly to the 12 major themes. Click on any of these themes to move into the specially designed page for that aspect of your story. You'll be able to add all of the important things in your life onto these pages.

Your story will have more than just a few words. You can draw together a collection of sights and sounds for each person, place, or thing. For example, in the My Work page you'll add the name of a job and the time you did that work, but one picture may not cover many years. To solve that problem, clicking on the *More* button will allow you to add more pictures and captions to tell the whole story. Therefore, each part of the *My Story* program has the potential to store an unlimited amount of information.

My Story home page
This is the main screen you'll see when you start *My Story*. From this point you can browse everything you've already added. And you can add as much material as you can fit on your computer.

Editable introduction
You can set the tone for your story. If you want to change the subtitle, simply click here and edit the introductory words.

Buttons
Each of the 12 buttons takes you to one of the categories that will inspire you to include every detail of your story.

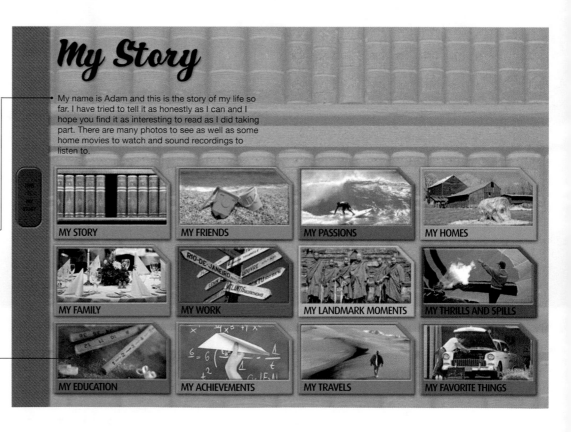

My name is Adam and this is the story of my life so far. I have tried to tell it as honestly as I can and I hope you find it as interesting to read as I did taking part. There are many photos to see as well as some home movies to watch and sound recordings to listen to.

MY STORY   MY FRIENDS   MY PASSIONS   MY HOMES

MY FAMILY   MY WORK   MY LANDMARK MOMENTS   MY THRILLS AND SPILLS

MY EDUCATION   MY ACHIEVEMENTS   MY TRAVELS   MY FAVORITE THINGS

My Work page

This page appears when you click the *My Work* button, listing your experience to date. You can add more entries using the *New* button at the top of the screen.

Main tools

These buttons allow you to perform actions quickly. The far left button creates a new blank record, while the others allow you to navigate records you have already added.

My Work

	Employer:	Date started:	...Until:
	Bricklayers, Inc.	05/12/1973	04/26/1974
	Location: Concord, MA		
	Hargreaves Accountants	04/29/1974	01/15/1976
	Location: Lexington, MA		
	Tiny Taxis	01/16/1976	05/25/1977
	Location: Winchester, MA		
	Pete's Photography	06/06/1977	08/09/1985
	Location: Boston, MA		
	Parks and Recreation Board	10/10/1985	03/02/1991
	Location: Birmingham, AL		
	Brian's Boats	05/04/1999	05/01/1997
	Location: Birmingham, England		
	Ricky's Computer Workshop	06/02/1998	09/05/1999

MY STORY	MY FRIENDS	MY PASSIONS	MY HOMES
MY FAMILY	**MY WORK**	MY LANDMARK MOMENTS	MY THRILLS AND SPILLS
MY EDUCATION	MY ACHIEVEMENTS	MY TRAVELS	MY FAVORITE THINGS

Detail button

This button leads you further into the story, where you can add more information about the job, as well as see a larger version of the media file (in this case, a photograph).

Media thumbnail

To add a media file, click on the *Add new file* button (see page 16) to the upper left of the record. The files are automatically adjusted in size to fit the box.

Shortcuts bar

You can jump quickly to any other chapter of your story with this handy *Shortcuts* button bar. It saves going back to the *Main menu* every time you want to change something.

Enlarge photo button
This button takes you to a larger view of the photo as shown on the opposite page. In this larger view, there is room to add more information about the time and place the photo was taken.

Editable information
Of course, you'll want to include a little bit of history, such as how you met your friend. There is plenty of room to add some interesting information.

My Friends

Sort by first name   Sort by last name

| Name (first/last): | Nick | Richardson | Nickname: | Speedy |
| Introduction: | A friend from my college fraternity |

| Name (first/last): | Tarquin | Smith | Nickname: | Boots |
| Introduction: | The captain of the football team I play with |

| Name (first/last): | Elizabeth | Davies | Nickname: | Libby |
| Introduction: | My college roommate's sister |

| Name (first/last): | Jemima | Patrickson | Nickname: | Gem |
| Introduction: | Member of my book club |

| Name (first/last): | Marie | Burnham | Nickname: | Firey |
| Introduction: | Met in the hospital when I had my appendix removed |

| Name (first/last): | Colin | Summer | Nickname: | Col |
| Introduction: | The owner of my local café |

THIS IS MY STORY

MY STORY	**MY FRIENDS**	MY PASSIONS	MY HOMES
MY FAMILY	MY WORK	MY LANDMARK MOMENTS	MY THRILLS AND SPILLS
MY EDUCATION	MY ACHIEVEMENTS	MY TRAVELS	MY FAVORITE THINGS

Add new file button
Clicking this button allows you to add a picture, video, or audio file of your choice to illustrate the record. When you click, a pop-up box will ask you what type of file you would like to import. Learn more about these files in Chapter 2.

All good things…
If you accidentally create an entry or want to get rid of one, you can simply click here to delete it. Don't worry—you'll be given a warning before the information is removed.

Play sound file
The caption title for this page is automatically generated by *My Story* from the information you provided in the previous page (opposite).

Captivating detail
There is plenty of space available for you to add a caption or anecdote for your picture or media file. You can provide as much detail as you like.

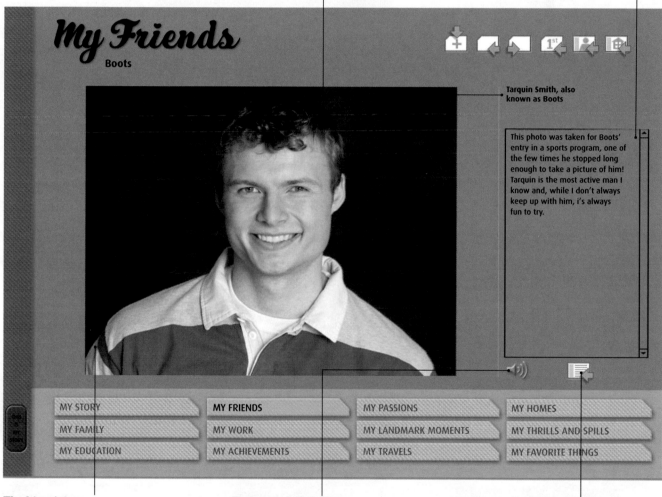

My Friends
Boots

Tarquin Smith, also known as Boots

This photo was taken for Boots' entry in a sports program, one of the few times he stopped long enough to take a picture of him! Tarquin is the most active man I know and, while I don't always keep up with him, i's always fun to try.

MY STORY	MY FRIENDS	MY PASSIONS	MY HOMES
MY FAMILY	MY WORK	MY LANDMARK MOMENTS	MY THRILLS AND SPILLS
MY EDUCATION	MY ACHIEVEMENTS	MY TRAVELS	MY FAVORITE THINGS

The big picture
Each picture can be seen at its largest size in the picture view.

Play sound file
If you have added an audio file rather than a picture or video file, click here to play it.

Return to list view
Pressing this button returns you to the previous page—in this case, the list view on the opposite page.

Source material

2

In this digital age you have other options besides jotting your story into a journal and gluing in the occasional Polaroid picture. The *My Story* program can help you draw on the wealth of files you store on your computer, including photographs, video, and more. If you're familiar with these kinds of files, you'll probably be itching to start, in which case you can jump to page 46.

If you'd prefer to get better acquainted with these digital files at a relaxed pace—not to mention pick up some tips on converting your older formats— then this is the chapter for you.

Digital cameras

The speed at which digital photography has established itself is a reflection of the huge technological and practical leap it has been for every photographer—from the humble hobbyist recording a vacation to the seasoned professional with demanding deadlines. Everyone who uses a digital camera has gained the advantage of instant results, both in terms of a camera playback screen and the ability to immediately transfer shots to a computer or printer.

Digital cameras also offer a range of additional features, such as the ability to record video clips—sometimes with sound—which can also be downloaded to your computer. In either case, and from whichever model, you'll discover that the files can be quickly added as you create your story using the *My Story* program.

Compact camera
Compact digital cameras are much smaller than their film equivalents, and they also contain many more features. This is because they're not restricted to the physical dimensions of a film format, and they do not need a mechanism to transport the film. These cameras are highly automated, allowing you to use the whole screen as a viewfinder. You simply need to press the shutter-release button to take a well-exposed picture.

High-end consumer camera

For an enthusiast who doesn't want to be restricted to the camera's automatic options, high-end consumer models offer increased manual control over the aperture and shutter speed settings and sometimes they offer the possibility to add an accessory flash. If you like this level of control, choose a model that includes shooting modes such as aperture priority rather than generic settings such as landscape, portrait, and sports modes.

Single Lens Reflex camera

For the ultimate in photographic quality and flexibility, a Single Lens Reflex (SLR) camera is the choice of amateurs and professionals alike. These cameras feature interchangeable lenses to give a huge range of shooting possibilities, from fish-eye wide angle to long telephoto zooms. They also tend to have many more controls, making it possible for the photographer to quickly make adjustments to the settings for the perfect shot.

HELP DESK

Although digital SLRs are excellent cameras, they lack the ability to record video like their compact brethren. That's because an SLR camera has a mechanical shutter that cannot be fired more than 10 times a second, even on the newest models. However, the sensor chips are optimized for still images and produce better quality photographs.

Scanners and scanning

For a project like *My Story*, the scanner's ability to convert old photographic prints from film into digital data is invaluable.

Even with this fantastic flexibility, scanners can be picked up for a relatively modest price, and even the cheapest model will produce great results in the My Story program.

The process of scanning varies slightly depending on the software that comes with the scanner, but the essential steps are the same.

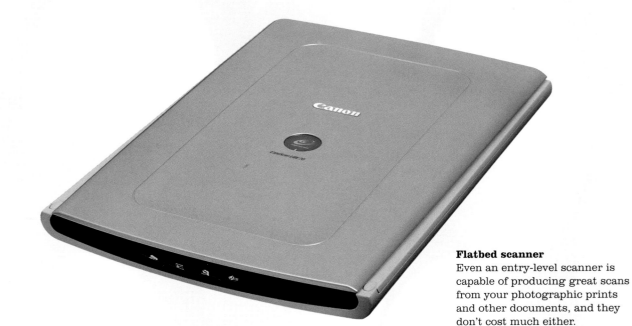

Flatbed scanner
Even an entry-level scanner is capable of producing great scans from your photographic prints and other documents, and they don't cost much either.

1 Be sure that your scanner is connected to the computer and it is switched on. Place your photograph face down on the glass platen and close the lid.

2 Open your scanning program and choose the *Preview* option. The scanner will quickly make a low-resolution scan.

3 If it does not select the photograph automatically, click on the image and drag the edges of the selection rectangle around the area you wish to scan.

4 Be sure you have selected the appropriate mode, such as *Photo* or *24-Bit Color*. Choose a reasonably low resolution, such as 100 ppi, to minimize the storage space you will need.

5 Finally, click *Scan* and, when the scanner is finished, chose *Save As....* From the *Type* menu pick "JPEG" and save the file onto your computer.

If you have a flatbed scanner, you can use your scanner to photograph small objects by placing them carefully on the platen and covering them with a cloth.

Flatbed scanner
At left is a typical flatbed scanner. The image is placed on the glass platen. The components that read the image are beneath the platen, much like an office photocopier.

Film scanner
A dedicated film scanner only scans film.

SCANNER FEATURES

When choosing a scanner, the most important factor—certainly the one the manufacturers are most eager to highlight—is the resolution. The higher the resolution, the more readings per square inch of the subject you're scanning, so it is a more detailed scan. This resolution is measured in Pixels Per Inch (PPI).

Another key statistic is density range, which is essentially a measurement of how subtle a difference the scanner can discern as shades approach white or black. A "DMax" figure of 4 or higher is good.

Other features to look for are the ability to scan film—usually achieved with a special adapter—and, of course, whether the included software is compatible with your computer.

Pictures on your computer

Photography has changed a lot in the last few years, but no change has been more significant than the switch from film to digital capture. Yet it is this change that makes a project like this possible—because if you could not convert pictures into digital information, you could not view them on your computer or add them to the *My Story* program.

That's not to say, however, that all of your photographs had to be taken with a digital camera. If that were the case, you would be confined to a very short period of time, because the first digital cameras only began to emerge at the beginning of the 1990s. Luckily, there are a number of ways to convert older photographs, depending on whether you're working with prints, slides, or something else. This book will help explain the methods, but first it's good to understand the basics of digital photo files.

JPEG settings

Original=616 KB   JPEG 100%=316 KB   JPEG 50%=168 KB   JPEG 1%=136 KB

It is possible to set different quality settings when you save JPEG files. The highest setting is 100 percent, and it loses the least detail from the original. As you can see, the file size—measured in kilobytes (KB)—decreases as the JPEG compression increases.

FILE TYPES

Computers store files—such as letters, photos, and songs—in specialized formats, each with its own characteristics. If you're used to writing letters using Microsoft Office, for example, you probably use the Word Document (.DOC) file format. However, for all formats, it all boils down to a series of zeros and ones.

To distinguish the meaning of one sequence from another, files introduce themselves by having different icons or alternative extensions—the series of letters after their names. Photograph files are similar. A few file types dominate the market, as explained below.

TYPE	DESCRIPTION	EXTENSION
JPEG	This is the most common format for digital cameras because it was specially designed to reduce the file size as much as possible, making it possible to fit more on a memory card. This is achieved by discarding some detail, but most cameras allow you to choose how much.	.jpg/.Jpeg
TIFF	This file type is the choice of most professionals because there is no compression. However, by preserving all of the image data, the files are much larger than JPEGs with the same number of pixels.	.tif/.tiff
RAW	This is not a single format, but rather a container for all of the information recorded by the camera as the shutter is released—not just the image sensor, but all of the other camera features, too.	.crw (Canon) .nef (Nikon)

The process of getting these more detailed files to the *My Story* program is analogous to working in the darkroom—you have greater flexibility to alter the tone or look of your images, but you need software to do it. This software is normally supplied with the camera because the raw data from one camera model is not the same as the next. You'll also find that different manufacturers use their own extensions for Raw files.

Computers store files in a hierarchy of folders, in which photographs can get easily lost among all of the documents finding their way onto computers these days. Apple, Microsoft, and others have come up with ways to make things a little easier. In many cases, as soon as you plug in a camera or scanner, a handy cataloging utility will take over, storing your images safely away from your other files where they're easy to find, show, and share. In addition, it will organize your pictures according to the time the photo was taken and other details recorded at the time of shooting. This information is known as metadata.

These are nice features, but you may need to find the original files from time to time—especially when copying them to your *My Story* project.

Other software

If you have installed an alternative program to take charge of your photographs, it might take over responsibility for the connection to your camera as well. This is normally your choice, but it's all too easy to unintentionally grant this access in the excitement of installing a program. In general, however, dedicated software is very useful. For example, Photoshop Elements 5 automatically opens a box offering the chance to rename your pictures as you upload them from the camera and the option to clear the camera's memory to be ready for your next shoot.

Next Photoshop Elements will open the images in its browser, which—much like Windows Photo Gallery or iPhoto on the opposite page—allows you to look through the images, apply tags and ratings, and perform simple corrections. It will also create a subfolder of the photos inside the "Pictures" folder on your computer so the photos are accessible from other Windows software. If you cannot locate the "Pictures" folder, the foolproof method is to save your photographs somewhere else using *File>Export*, which will make a copy at the location of your choice.

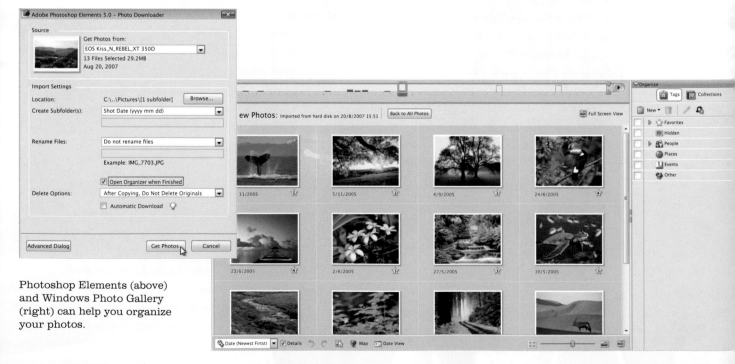

Photoshop Elements (above) and Windows Photo Gallery (right) can help you organize your photos.

WINDOWS PHOTO GALLERY

Windows Vista (Home Edition version and higher) includes Windows Photo Gallery, which is a convenient tool for scrolling through your photographs. It groups your photos around the date they were taken, and allows you to give your pictures star ratings, making it easier to find the best ones as your collection expands. The pictures are, by default, positioned in your computer's "Pictures" folder, which can be easily accessed from other programs.

iPHOTO

The iPhoto utility, included with every Apple Macintosh computer, automatically recognizes when you attach a digital camera and offers to download your images for you. You can then scroll through the files and make edits, but you cannot immediately access the images from other programs. To view them, you must:

 Open iPhoto and locate the photo you want by scrolling or clicking on one of the folders.

2 Click on your chosen picture to highlight it.

3 Click *File>Export* and, in the pop-up box, set the file type to JPEG.

 Click *Export* and choose a location on your computer to save the picture. If you plan to export many pictures, you may want to use the *New Folder* button to keep them organized in one place on your computer.

Music on your computer

The rise of digital music has been unstoppable in recent years, especially since it was popularized by portable MPEG Audio Layer 3 (MP3) players such as Apple's phenomenally successful iPod. But MP3 technology doesn't just live in portable players. An MP3 is a digital file that is just as at home on a computer. Most portable music players are virtually useless without their accompanying computer media player.

These programs—such as iTunes and Windows Media Player—take advantage of your computer's power and Internet connection so you can copy your CDs into your music library and buy new music. They are also incredibly useful tools on their own, making it really easy to sort through your music and play the tune you want. Better still, if you don't already have one of these tools on your computer, iTunes, for example, can be downloaded for free for both Mac and Windows PCs.

COMMON MUSIC FILE TYPES

MP3 This is the most common music file format, and it works with Windows Media Player, iTunes, and virtually all portable players (including the iPod). This is the recommended format for the *My Story* program.

AAC Advanced Audio Coding is the standard file type for iTunes and the iTunes store.

WMA Windows Media Audio is Microsoft's alternative to MP3 and AAC files. It is compatible with its media player and less popular digital music platforms.

iPod
Portable music players such as the iPod have kick-started the digital-music revolution. If you have one of these, there is a good chance you already have MP3 files on your computer.

Windows Media Player
You'll find much of the same functionality as iTunes in Microsoft's Windows Media Player, although the latter is only available for Windows.

View
Choose the way the music is organized on the screen to suit your taste: list, album, band, or covers.

Sort
Click on the top of any column to sort all of the music alphabetically (or numerically) based on that column. Click a second time to reverse the direction (so a–z becomes z–a).

Search
Type the name (or part of a name) of a specific artist, album, or tune to find it instantly.

Store
The *Store* option switches to a store page. This allows you to browse and buy new music through the Internet.

Info
The computer uses this area to display information about the track currently playing, just like a stereo.

Radio
Internet radio is streamed to your computer over the Internet and, just like a regular radio, the signals are not recorded. Click the menu to see a list of channels.

iTunes Coverflow
If you switch to the *Coverflow* view, you can pick a tune by scrolling through the album cover artwork.

Import
When there is a CD in the computer's drive, iTunes offers to copy it, or rip it, onto the computer (see page 30).

Playlists
A list of tunes that the computer will play in order. You can add to it by dragging files from the main catalog view and rearranging the order.

Catalog
This list switches to different parts of the catalog so you can view or hear files that are already on your computer.

Copying music from a CD

Along with the calculator, the CD was the most successful digital product to enter the home. If you have an extensive CD collection, your music is already in digital form, which makes the process of including it into your *My Story* project much easier.

However, there are still a few steps to take. Despite predating MP3s by some time, a CD actually stores much more digital information about the music. That's great if quality is your only concern, but by using lossy compression—discarding certain details that the human ear finds hard to discern—MP3s allow you to make much better use of limited hard drive (or iPod) space. Conveniently, we can use the same software that creates MP3s with the *My Story* program.

HELP DESK

When it is installed, iTunes automatically creates a folder, or directory, on your computer's hard drive where it stores all of your music. This is conveniently organized into folders by artist, then album name, so it's easy to browse through it using Windows Explorer, Mac OS X Finder, or any application's *File>Open...* box. The only potential problem is you may not be able to find the folder!

The default locations are within your "Music" folder (Users/[your name]/Music/iTunes) if you're using a Mac. In Windows it is C:/Users/[your name]/Music/iTunes. You can, however, change this in the *Advanced Preferences* options.

Screenshot 1 (Advanced Preferences)

Advanced

General | Podcasts | Playback | Sharing | Store | Advanced | Parental | Apple TV | Syncing

General | Importing | Burning

On CD Insert: Ask To Import CD

Import Using: MP3 Encoder

Setting: High Quality (160 kbps)

Details
80 kbps (mono)/160 kbps (stereo), joint stereo, optimized for MMX/SSE, using MP.

☑ Play songs while importing or converting
☑ Automatically retrieve CD track names from Internet
☑ Create file names with track number
☑ Use error correction when reading Audio CDs

Use this option if you experience problems with the audio quality from Audio CDs. This may reduce the speed of importing.

Note: These settings do not apply to songs downloaded from the iTunes Store.

1 Open iTunes and click *iTunes>Preferences* (Mac) or *Fdit>Preferences* (Windows). Choose *Advanced* from the top. Next select the *Importing* tab. Set the *Import Using* option to *MP3* and click *OK*.

Screenshot 2 (iTunes Accessing Gracenote)

View | Store | Advanced | Window | Help

iTunes

Accessing Gracenote CDDB@
Getting Track Names...

Forty Licks (Disc 2)
The Rolling Stones

Name	Time
☑ Start Me Up	3:33
☑ Brown Sugar	3:49
☑ Miss You	3:35

2 Insert an audio CD and wait a few moments for the computer to recognize it. If you are connected to the Internet, iTunes will briefly scan an online database for information about the CD.

Screenshot 3 (iTunes Importing)

View | Store | Advanced | Window | Help

iTunes

Importing "You Never Give Me Your Money"
Time remaining: 0:10 (9.3x)

	Name	Time	Artist
1	Come Together	4:20	The Beatles
2	Something	3:03	The Beatles
3	Maxwell's Silver Hammer	3:27	The Beatles
4	Oh! Darling	3:26	The Beatles
5	Octopus's Garden	2:51	The Beatles
6	I Want You (She's So Heavy)	7:47	The Beatles
7	Here Cames The Sun	3:05	The Beatles
8	Because	2:45	The Beatles
9	You Never Give Me Your Money	4:02	The Beatles
10	Sun King	2:26	The Beatles
11	Mean Mr.Mustard	1:06	The Beatles
12	Polythene Pam	1:12	The Beatles
13	She Came In Through The Bath...	1:57	The Beatles

3 Click on the *Import* button and wait while the computer copies the tunes into its database—at this point they are converted to MP3 files. When the computer has finished, eject the CD.

Screenshot 4 (iTunes folder)

iTunes

Album Artwork | iTunes Library | iTunes Music

iTunes Music Library.xml | Previous iTunes Libraries

4 You can now access the files through iTunes, but they will also be stored in your computer's iTunes folder (see Help Desk, page 30). You can copy them from this folder for use in other programs, including the *My Story* program.

Copying older recordings

Despite the prevalence of digital music, both on CDs and devices such as the iPod, many of us still keep a collection of cherished vinyl or well-worn cassette tapes. These are analog mediums that record sound vibrations mechanically, in a way that might seem more natural to the human mind (and ear, according to many purists). But this format is difficult for computers to comprehend.

That said, sound is essentially an analog experience, and the computer has no trouble taking digital information from CDs or DVD soundtracks and sending it to our ears. All we need to do is reverse the process. Luckily, most computers already have a built-in solution to this problem, in the form of a line-in socket.

YOU WILL NEED
- A record or cassette player

- An RCA to 3.5 mm stereo jack lead or a 3.5 mm to 3.5 mm stereo jack lead

- A sound recording program, such as Sound Recorder (Windows) or GarageBand (Mac)

- A line-in socket

THE BEATLES

USB TURNTABLES

An easy-to-use solution is a Universal Serial Bus (USB) turntable. This turntable plugs directly into your computer's USB socket and allows you to record music directly into standard computer formats such as MP3 (see page 28). This popular model is compatible with both Mac and Windows PCs.

 Locate your computer's line-in socket. Its appearance varies depending on the make and model of your computer, but generally it is a 3.5 mm socket, similar to one used in a portable music player's headphone socket.

 Locate your record or cassette player's line-out socket. This will either be a 3.5 mm socket or a pair of RCA phono sockets.

3 Connect the devices using the appropriate cable (see You Will Need box on page 32).

4 Start your sound recording program. Be sure it is connected to the line-in socket (otherwise it might try and record from a built-in microphone). Begin recording.

5 Play your record or cassette.

6 Stop both once your recording is finished.

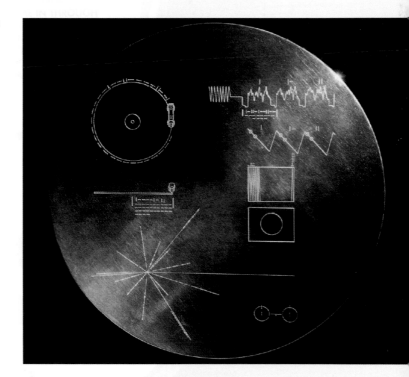

The Voyager record
Records were highly regarded by NASA, who famously made a golden disc for each of the Voyager probes. Each disc included sounds and video reflecting aspects of humanity in a format that could be understood by any alien race discovering the craft as it drifted across the galaxy.

Make your own recording

There are many reasons why you may want to make your own recordings—from sampling your own voice to laying down your big musical number for posterity. In any case, you'll find any modern computer capable of making these recordings without any additional equipment. An external microphone usually provides better quality, but if your computer has one built in it will usually be more than adequate and very convenient.

A microphone picks up sound vibrations from the air and turns them into electronic impulses. The computer translates these impulses into a digital signal that can be saved as a computer file. By reducing the distance the sound has to travel through the air, and minimizing background noise, you will get the best quality.

USB Mic
This microphone plugs directly into the computer's USB socket, providing a direct digital signal. These are especially useful for laptop computers that don't have a microphone or line-in socket.

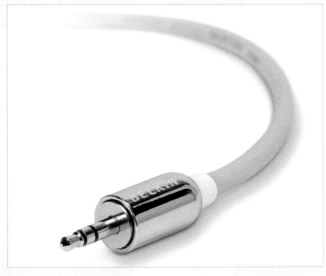

1 If you are using an external microphone, make sure it is correctly connected to your computer. A USB microphone can be connected to any USB socket. However, a traditional 3.5 mm plug is easily confused with a line-out or headphone socket, so be sure you use the right one.

2 Open your computer's *Control Panel* (or *System Preferences* window on a Mac) and choose the *Sound* option. There will be an *Input* option—be sure that your microphone (or line-in) is selected.

Sound

Playback | Recording | Sounds

Select a recording device below to modify its settings:

Microphone
Realtek AC'97 Audio
Working

Line In
Realtek AC'97 Audio
Currently unavailable

Configure | Set Default | Properties

OK | Cancel | Apply

Microphone Properties

General | Custom | Levels | Advanced

Microphone

Change Icon...

Controller Information

Realtek AC'97 Audio
Realtek

Properties

Jack Information

No Jack Information Available

Device usage: Use this device (enable)

OK | Cancel | Apply

3 Now switch to a recording program. Many versions of Windows include a simple sound recorder in the "Accessories" folder, which is suitable.

Sound Recorder

■ Stop Recording   00:00:36

4 Click *Record* to begin the recording, and *Stop Recording* to finish it.

Save As

« Users ▸ Adam ▸ Documents ▸   Search

File name: My Sound Recording

Save as type: Window Media Audio File

Artists: Specify contributing art...   Artists: Specify album

Browse Folders   Save

5 In Windows, the *Save* box will automatically appear when you have finished recording. Choose a name and click *OK*. (If you're using GarageBand, you will need to click *File>Export*.)

GARAGEBAND

All Apple computers include a full-featured music-sequencing program that also has the ability to record. If you're recording yourself playing a musical instrument, this is the ideal tool, but it can also be used to make a simple voice recording. Open the program and choose a male or female voice from the side panel before clicking the red *Record* button. When you've finished, click *File>Export* and save the recording as an MP3 file.

Video on your computer

Pictures and sound are both more than comfortable on modern computers, so it won't come as a surprise that video has made the jump to digital, too. The ubiquity of the Digital Versatile Disc (DVD) serves as evidence of this fact. However, free from the shackles of television's very definite specifications, video on a computer can appear in all shapes and (file) sizes—from postage-stamp sized cell-phone clips to widescreen High Definition (HD). While flexibility can be a blessing, it is also something of a hindrance, because it means there are numerous file formats involved.

To simplify matters, the *My Story* program uses the Apple QuickTime player. It is installed as a standard program on all Macintosh computers and many Windows computers. If you are using Windows and you are not sure whether you have QuickTime installed, follow the instructions on page 37.

QuickTime program
When you've finished installing QuickTime, you will be able to find the player in your computer's *Programs* area. A shortcut may also appear on your desktop, which you can trash without deleting the player program.

COMMON VIDEO FILES

TYPE	DESCRIPTION	EXTENSION
QuickTime	A group of formats that are popular because many can be played over the Internet on different computer systems. It includes resolutions up to full High Definition.	.mov
Windows Media	A Windows-only video format. You will need to convert WMV files to a QuickTime-compatible format to use them with *My Story*.	.wmv

HELP DESK

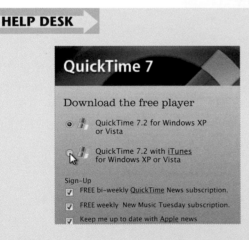

You can choose to download and install iTunes at the same time as QuickTime. iTunes is the program used to create digital sound files as shown on page 30.

If no video appears in this box, you will need to install Quicktime

Click here to download the latest version

1 Insert the CD included with this book and proceed to the menu page. You will need to agree to the terms and conditions. Select the *Test for QuickTime* button.

2 Your Internet browser will be launched, and a small video will begin playing if you have QuickTime installed. If not, you will see an error message.

3 Follow the link beneath the error message to download the latest version of QuickTime. This may take a few minutes, but it will be much faster if you have a broadband connection.

4 Once the QuickTime installer appears, follow the on-screen instructions.

Digital video cameras

Most video cameras now available are digital, which means there will be a way to transfer video to your computer and, by extension, the *My Story* program. There are essentially three different kinds of video camera, which all work in slightly different ways.

The most established digital format is MiniDV, which is now more than 10 years old. It was designed to be a computer-friendly format, and most cameras include a Firewire connection (also known as iLink or IEEE 1394). Your computer can use this connection to control the camera to play and copy the tape. Apple's iMovie and Windows Movie Maker can do this and they are included with their respective computer systems.

Video cassettes
Many video cameras use cassettes that can store very high-quality digital video. Although 60 minutes does not sound long, it requires many gigabytes of computer storage space.

iMovie
When you connect your camera, each video clip is copied to your computer. Drag them into the project timeline to make them part of the final video.

If you're one of the many users who enjoy the convenience of a direct-to-DVD camcorder, you are not excluded from computer editing. Even if the camera doesn't have a direct USB or Firewire computer link, there is always the possibility of copying the video from the DVD (see page 42) to your hard disk drive.

Finally, there are cameras that record onto a hard disk drive or another form of digital memory, which can be downloaded without waiting for the cassette drive. The process of copying to your computer is as simple as connecting it—usually via USB—and copying the files from the disk, as you would with a handheld digital camera.

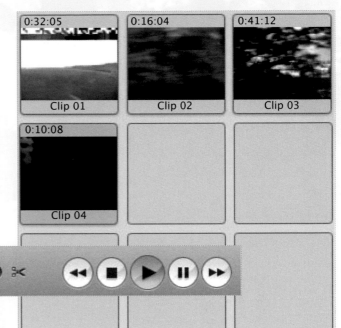

Firewire
Firewire connectors come in two standard shapes: small 4-pin connectors that are common on cameras and large connectors that are common on a computer. Your electronics retailer will be able to supply you with a cable that fits your equipment.

HDD camcorder
Hard Disk-based cameras do not have a slot to insert media because they simply record onto a built-in hard drive. To preserve your memories, you must copy them from the disk or the space will run out.

DVD camcorder
It's usually easy to recognize a DVD camcorder by its circular disk drive.

Other camera devices

Although there are a wide variety of camcorders, they are not the only way video is recorded these days. Most compact digital cameras—including those in camera phones—are capable of recording video of some kind. These multipurpose devices might not achieve the same quality as dedicated camcorders and they often lack the space to store large video files, but there is enough detail to bring a favorite memory to life.

The best way to retrieve video files varies from device to device, but generally you can copy the video clips the same way you would transfer photos. This means attaching the camera, phone, or device using a USB cable and copying them, or swapping the memory card from the camera to a memory-card reader on the computer. If both devices have Bluetooth wireless connectivity, however, it's possible to work without cables, as shown on page 41.

Extreme cameras
Some video cameras that are designed to record extreme sports produce too much vibration to record on anything except memory cards. These cameras work more like still cameras when it comes to transferring your files.

MICRO MEMORY CARDS

Both the Memory Stick and Secure Digital (SD) memory-card ranges now include special micro versions, similar in size to a small fingernail, which take up less space in devices such as mobile phones. To read these cards you usually need a special adapter that is the same size as a standard Memory Stick or SD Card. If your card wasn't supplied with one, you can find one at a phone retailer.

1 The first time you connect your computer and phone, you'll need to set them up so they recognize each other. You can do this by enabling Bluetooth on both devices so they are transmitting. Use your computer's *System Preferences* or *Control Panel* menu.

2 Make sure that both devices are within 10 feet (3 m) of each other and set to *Discoverable*. Now they will be able to recognize each other and exchange basic information.

3 Open your computer's *Control Panel* or *System Preferences* window. Choose *Set Up Bluetooth Device* on your computer and wait while the computer scans for working Bluetooth devices. When your phone appears on the list, click on it.

4 Follow the on-screen instructions. You will usually be asked to type a code from the computer screen into the phone for security.

5 From this point on, whenever the computer and phone are in range and Bluetooth is switched on, you will be able to browse through the files in the phone's memory and copy them to the computer by clicking *Browse Device*.

Bluetooth dongle
If your computer does not have Bluetooth wireless capability, you can purchase this inexpensive device and attach it to one of the USB sockets. You can then transfer files from a Bluetooth-capable cell phone without a cable.

Copying from a DVD

Copying video from a DVD is not always an easy process, usually because your computer often assumes that you want to watch the disc. It will helpfully switch to a DVD-playing application and often take up the whole screen. Another problem is that DVDs store a great deal of information per second in a format designed to look the best on television screens rather than computer monitors. However, if you've committed a special memory to a DVD and you want to copy it into *My Story*, there are a few solutions. The best involves converting the digital files on the disc to a digital format better suited for computer use. The only real downside is the process is very demanding, so it can take a while.

1 Insert your DVD and quit any DVD Player application that launched automatically.

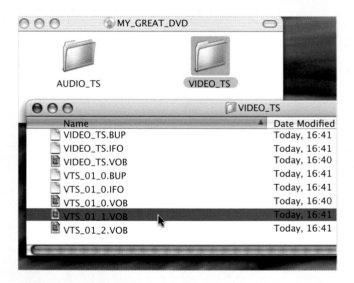

RIGHTS MANAGEMENT

If you create your own DVDs, chances are that they will be free of rights management, so you will be able to convert the files. Commercial discs, however, often use digital encryption (known as Digital Rights Management or DRM) to prevent their use in this way.

2 Using the *Finder* (Mac) or *Explorer* (Windows), locate and open the "VIDEO_TS" folder on the DVD. This will be located at the top of the DVD's file structure.

3 This folder contains the component parts of the DVD, which are recorded as large files. Open one of these in the QuickTime player.

4 Scroll along the movie quickly by dragging the play head (the downward-pointing triangle in the timeline beneath the movie) until you find the section you'd like to copy into *My Story*. If you can't find it, try another large file from the "VIDEO_TS" folder.

5 Press "I" to mark an "in point" at the beginning of the section you want to keep. Locate the end of the section with the play head, and press "O" to set the "out point."

6 To trim the movie to the required size, click *Edit>Trim to Selection*.

7 Finally, to save the image in a more compact, computer-friendly format, click *File>Export* and choose *Broadband–Medium* from the drop-down menu. Save the file in a convenient location and wait while the movie is saved.

Copying from video or cine

Whether your favorite moments of footage have been recorded onto celluloid—perhaps using an old 8 mm cine camera—or have ended up on one of the many video-cassette formats that pre-date digital, getting them onto your computer requires special equipment.

In the case of video, the equipment is known as an Analog to Digital converter, and you can either purchase one or use the services of a dedicated agency. If you are using cine film—which will probably have had at least 30 years to age—you will find yourself restricted to using an agency. Home equipment can be found, but it is certainly not for the fainthearted. If you do go to an agency, be prepared to pay per foot of film, but remember that converting your film doesn't mean you can use it just in the *My Story* program. You'll also be able to use it in other digital projects, including a DVD or even a Web site.

Connects to computer's USB2 socket.

Analog to Digital converter
A cost-effective solution for converting video—assuming you have a suitable video-cassette player or camcorder—is to use a converter such as the Plextor Convertex above. You can record video directly from your player or camcoder with the supplied software.

Connects to an S-Video source

Connects to a stereo audio source

Connects to a composite video source

Cine film projector
This Heurtier model is a typical home-movie projector from before the days of digital camcorders and LCD television screens. Professionals can convert cine film using specially adapted projector-camera devices.

DIGITAL 8

If you have a large collection of Video 8 home movies, it might be worth looking for a Digital 8 camera, although you might need to go to yard sales to find one. Digital 8 cameras feature the same digital technology as MiniDV cameras, but record onto Video 8-sized cassettes.

In other words, you have all the advantages of digital—from the computer's perspective the results are indistinguishable—with the added ability to play your old tapes, too. Some models are even able to produce a digital signal for a computer connected by Firewire when playing an analog tape, making them ideal for converting Video 8 tapes to digital.

Telling your story

3

Think of the *My Story* program as your muse—
a series of creative screens that will empower and
inspire you to capture the details of your favorite
memories that make up the story of your life. Just as
a poet's muse shatters writer's block, using *My Story*
will prevent you from wondering what to say next.
Meanwhile, it will catalog your memories about
your friends, family, work, travels, achievements,
and more, in a format that is both simple to browse
and easy on the eye. This chapter will help you
choose your memories and use the program to its
full potential.

Installing on Windows

Before you can use the *My Story* program, you will need to install it on your computer. This process is very easy thanks to the automated installer program included on the disc, but there are still some points that you should consider.

It is a good idea to follow the steps on this page methodically, especially if you are not familiar with adding programs to your computer.

HELP DESK

Many Windows users choose to disable the "AutoRun" feature. However, you may find that when you put the *My Story* disc into your computer, nothing happens. To begin the *My Story* Installer, you must click the *Start* button and choose "My Computer" or *Accessories>Windows Explorer*. From there you should be able to find the CD drive.

1 Insert the *My Story* CD-ROM into your computer's CD-ROM drive. You will need to wait a few seconds after inserting the disc for the drive to "spin up." In other words, the disc begins to spin inside the computer so that information can be read from it. Unless you have disabled *AutoRun* in your *Control Panel* (see box), Windows will automatically launch the *My Story* program. In some cases, your computer will detect that the program is attempting to launch and ask your permission. In that case, click OK. You should reach the start screen with a license agreement.

2 Review the license agreement and, if you agree to the terms, click on the *I agree to the license* button to proceed. If you do not agree, you will not be able to use the program.

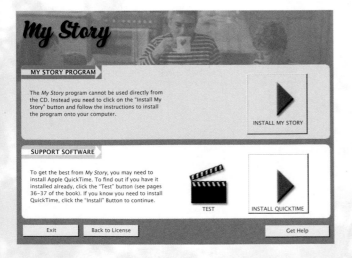

VIDEO AND AUDIO FILES

When you first run *My Story,* the program will automatically create a folder on your computer's main hard drive (the C: drive), where it will store copies of the video and audio files that you add. Do not delete these files.

My Story

MY STORY PROGRAM

The *MyStory* program cannot be used directly from the CD. Instead you need to click on the "Install My Story" button and follow the instructions to install the program onto your computer.

INSTALL MY STORY

SUPPORT SOFTWARE

To get the best from *MyStory*, you may need to install Apple QuickTime. To find out if you have it installed already, click the "Test" button (see pages 36–37 of the book). If you know you need to install QuickTime, click the "Install" Button to continue.

TEST

INSTALL QUICKTIME

| Exit | Back to License | Get Help |

Copy Files from CD to Hard Drive

Source Folder (CD)

C:\uers\public\myom_menu\mystory\cd_root\RESOURCE\My Story

Destination Folder

Browse Folder

Start Copy Process

File

Cancel

---

3 There are two options on the disc. The first allows you to install *My Story*. The second allows you to check and update the video playback program QuickTime, installed on your computer. To install *My Story*, click on the *Install My Story* button in the upper box.

4 A new window will appear with an empty field called "Destination Folder." You need to tell the computer a location on your hard disc to place the files. Do this by clicking the *Browse Folder* button.

Browse Folder

C:\Users\ilex users\Desktop

- Drives
  - Local Disk (C:)
    - Recycle Bin
    - Applications
    - ATI
    - Boot
    - Documents and Settings
    - EPSON
    - labd87ea5cc24d2000a84a
    - FlagsForKate
    - MSOCache
    - Program Files
    - Program Files (x86)
    - ProgrameData
    - System Volume Information
    - Temp
    - Users
    - Windows
  - DVD Drive (D:)
  - DVD RW Drive: (E:)

| Create Folder... | Ok | Cancel |

Copy Files from CD to Hard Drive

Source Folder (CD)

C:\uers\public\myom_menu\mystory\cd_root\RESOURCE\My Story

Destination Folder

C:\Users\ilex user\Desktop

Browse Folder

Start Copy Process

File

Cancel

---

5 A subwindow will appear, allowing you to choose the location to install *My Story*. Be sure to choose a location that you can easily find again. Click OK to return to the previous screen.

6 Be sure there is an address in the "Destination Folder" box, then click *Start Copy Process*. When finished, you will be offered the chance to open an Explorer window and see the copied files, including the *My Story* program. Double click on this to start using the program.

Installing on a Mac

Installing the *My Story* program on a Macintosh computer is very straightforward thanks to a simple drag-and-drop installer. Although this is the approach recommended for most circumstances, you may prefer to install it in another location elsewhere on your computer.

As long as you have not altered the location of the standard "Applications" folder, the installation process on a Mac is simple. If you have changed the "Application" folder's location, follow the advice in the Help Desk box (right) and do not use the alias in step 3.

HELP DESK

If your computer is set up with multiple user accounts, you might decide not to install *My Story* in the computer's "Applications" folder because it is shared between all of the accounts on your computer. Instead, you can simply drag the *My Story* folder to any location within your user area, such as the "Documents" folder or your desktop.

My Story CD

1 Insert the *My Story* CD-ROM into your computer's CD-ROM drive and wait a few seconds for the drive to "spin up," so the information can be read from it.

2 A *My Story CD* icon will appear on your computer desktop. Double click on it to open the *My Story* window.

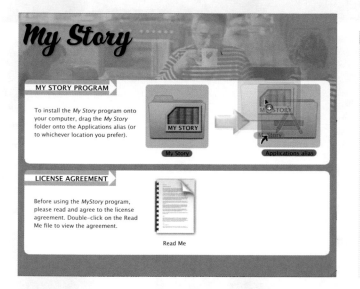

My Story

MY STORY PROGRAM

To install the *My Story* program onto your computer, drag the *My Story* folder onto the Applications alias (or to whichever location you prefer).

MY STORY

My Story

Applications alias

LICENSE AGREEMENT

Before using the *MyStory* program, please read and agree to the license agreement. Double-click on the Read Me file to view the agreement.

Read Me

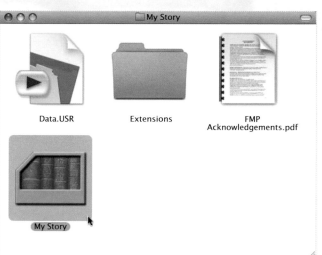

Data.USR   Extensions   FMP Acknowledgements.pdf

My Story

3 You will see two icons: a *My Story* folder and an alias to your "Applications" folder. For a standard install, simply drag the *My Story* folder onto the "Applications" folder alias to install *My Story* into your "Applications" folder.

4 To open *My Story*, open the "Applications" folder, then open the "*My Story*" folder within it. Double click on the *My Story* program to run it.

VIDEO AND AUDIO FILES

When you first run *My Story,* the program will automatically create a folder in your computer's main boot drive (the drive where your version of Mac OS X is stored). It will store copies of the video and audio files that you add to your version of the *My Story* program. Do not delete these files, or the video and audio files will be lost from your database. The photo files, however, are stored within the program.

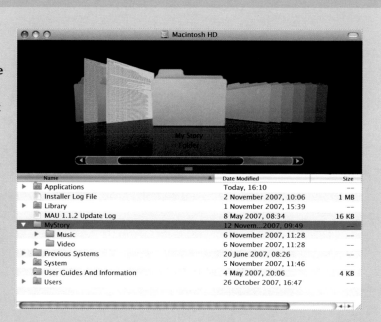

Name	Date Modified	Size
▶ Applications	Today, 16:10	--
Installer Log File	2 November 2007, 10:06	1 MB
▶ Library	1 November 2007, 15:39	--
MAU 1.1.2 Update Log	8 May 2007, 08:34	16 KB
▼ MyStory	12 Novem...2007, 09:49	--
▶ Music	6 November 2007, 11:28	--
▶ Video	6 November 2007, 11:28	--
▶ Previous Systems	20 June 2007, 08:26	--
▶ System	5 November 2007, 11:46	--
User Guides And Information	4 May 2007, 20:06	4 KB
▶ Users	26 October 2007, 16:47	--

Launching *My Story*

Once you have installed *My Story* onto your computer, you will not need the CD to launch the program. Instead you can open it as soon as you have started your operating system (Windows or Mac OS) from the location where you saved it.

Another trick to quickly start the program is to create a link, or alias, which can be placed on the desktop for quick access. This is a small file that tells the computer where to find the full copy of *My Story* that you have already transferred from the CD.

Windows

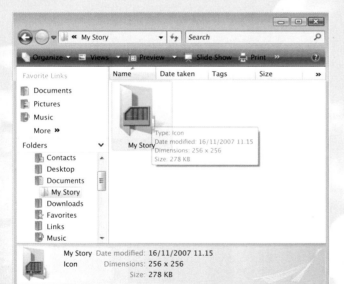

1 Once you have started Windows, you will need to find the files that you transferred with the installer program (see page 48). Use Windows Explorer—supplied with all versions of Windows—to locate the file. To launch, simply double click on it.

2 If you want to create a link, hold down the Alt key and drag *My Story* from Windows Explorer to your computer desktop. When you release the button, a link will appear. However, the *My Story* program will remain in its original location.

3 Close the Explorer window. From now on, all you need to do to launch *My Story* is double click on the link you just created.

Mac

1 Open a *Finder* window by clicking on the *Finder* icon to the far left of the dock or by clicking *File>New Finder Window*.

2 Click on the *Applications* shortcut in the sidebar, then scroll to locate the *"My Story"* folder.

3 To launch *My Story*, double click on the highlighted *My Story* application. The other supporting files need to be here, but you will not need to use them directly.

4 To create an alias, right click on the *My Story* application (Ctrl+click if you have a one-button mouse). A new alias file will appear in the same *Finder* window.

5 Now simply drag the alias file to your desktop. To launch the program, double click on the desktop alias.

Getting started

Just as every book has an introduction and every diary has a first page, the story of your life needs some opening words. Even if you never intend to share your story with anyone else, it will add a sense of purpose. On the other hand, if you want future generations to understand everything that has touched your life or everything that you include in your story, then it's essential to introduce yourself first.

HELP DESK

If you make a mistake, just click on the introduction again—at the point of the mistake—and edit the text as you did in step 4. You can also use the Cursor keys (with the arrows) to move around the box.

Many authors have been told that the first sentence needs to sum up the entire story, which is enough pressure to give a bestselling author a serious attack of writer's block.

Your beginning doesn't need to be so auspicious. All you need to do is introduce yourself—your name is a good start—and let *My Story* guide you through the rest.

1 The opening words of your story will appear on the *Main* menu page. To get there, open *My Story*—it's the first page that appears—or click to the page using the *Home* button.

2 Click on the area that reads "Enter your introduction here" and you will see a box appear. This means the area is live, and ready to be edited.

3 Triple click on the text to highlight it, then press the Delete key to remove it all at once.

My name is Adam Juniper and this is my story so far; the people I've met, the friends I've made, and the things that I consider important to me.

My name is Adam Juniper and this is my story so far; the people I've met, the friends I've made, and the things that I consider important to me. Within these 12 buttons you'll find pictures, sounds, and videos from me (and my friends). I hope you enjoy them as much as I have making this record of my life. Oh, and I'm not finished yet!

4 Type in your introduction. If you make a mistake, use the Backspace or Delete key to go back and retype.

5 When you have finished your introduction, move the mouse cursor to the empty area to the right (or any empty area of the screen) and click the mouse once.

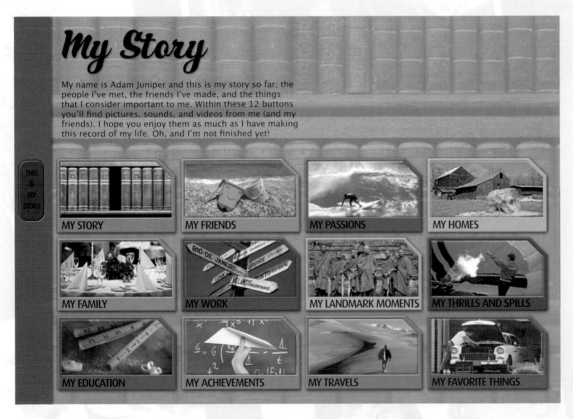

My Story

My name is Adam Juniper and this is my story so far; the people I've met, the friends I've made, and the things that I consider important to me. Within these 12 buttons you'll find pictures, sounds, and videos from me (and my friends). I hope you enjoy them as much as I have making this record of my life. Oh, and I'm not finished yet!

THIS IS MY STORY

MY STORY

MY FRIENDS

MY PASSIONS

MY HOMES

MY FAMILY

MY WORK

MY LANDMARK MOMENTS

MY THRILLS AND SPILLS

MY EDUCATION

MY ACHIEVEMENTS

MY TRAVELS

MY FAVORITE THINGS

The finished text introduces everything that is to come. As you build and enhance the details of your story, you can come back and tweak—or even rewrite—this introduction whenever you like.

Your story

While you can set the scene with a 90-word introduction, it's likely you'll have more to say, and the best place to say it is in the *My Story* section. This is your chance to flex your verbal muscles, tell the whole story of your life, and add some pictures to highlight those important memories.

Once you press the *My Story* button, you'll find two new screens: The first is waiting for all your juicy details, and the second is a photo list that will become very familiar as you build your story. While the choice of words is very much your own, here's how to import your pictures into *My Story*.

1 To get to the *My Story* section, click on the *My Story* button toward the top left of the *Main* menu page.

2 To edit the words in the *My Story* page, simply click on the text and add or delete as you did with the introduction (see page 55). When you're ready to add a picture, click on the *Pictures* button at the bottom of the text area.

3 When you first start, there will be no visible pictures, but a missing image logo has been placed to guide you. Click on the *Insert Media* icon to the left of the logo.

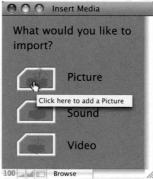

4 When you click on the *Insert Media* icon, a window will appear. Choose the type of media you want to insert—in this case you are adding a picture.

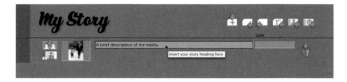

6 The picture will appear in the small thumbnail view. To add a caption, click in the caption box to the right and begin typing (see page 54).

5 The *Insert Picture* box will appear. This might look slightly different depending on your operating system, but the principle is the same. Locate the picture file on your computer system (see pages 26–27) and click OK.

7 You can add a date to the image by clicking on the *Date* input box and opening the calendar. To see the picture enlarged on your screen, click the *Picture View* button to the left of the thumbnail.

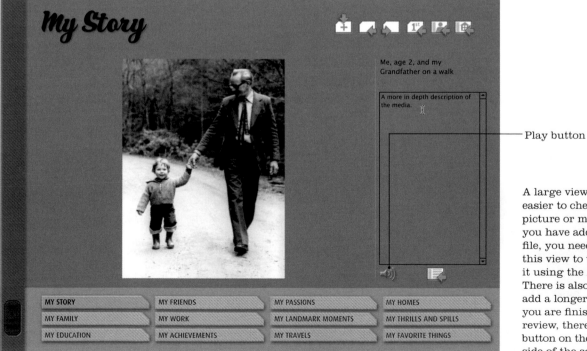

Play button

A large view makes it easier to check your picture or media file. If you have added a media file, you need to switch to this view to watch or hear it using the *Play* button. There is also a space to add a longer caption. Once you are finished with your review, there is a *Back* button on the lower right side of the screen.

Your friends

Your friends are probably an important part of your life, so you will want to do them justice. Some friends come and go, while others may have been with you for as long as you can remember. In either case, they have played their part in every stage of your life. The only real problem is remembering how you met everyone in your life. To make that as easy as possible, *My Story* doesn't require you to remember everyone at once. You can open the My Friends page at any time and add a new entry. If you're still having trouble, check the Writer's Block box on page 61 for some ideas to include in your captions.

Here's how to add a new friend to *My Story* when you open the program for the first time. On the following pages you'll see how you can expand on the information added here:

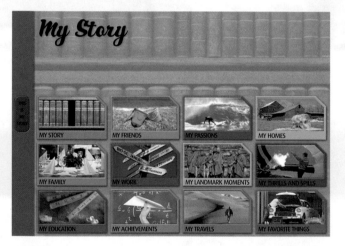

1 Once you've opened *My Story* (see page 52) you are presented with a number of different pages or sections. Click on the *My Friends* button to open the My Friends page.

2 The My Friends page is a list with room for more than one friend on the same page. When you start the program, however, there will be one empty record available at the top, which you should fill first.

3 To add a friend's details to the empty sections, click on the text boxes, delete the example text, and write your own instead (see page 54).

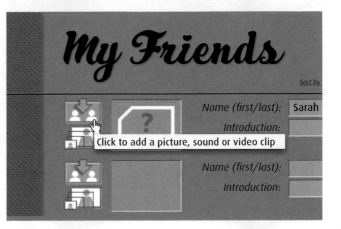

4

If you want to add more friends to the list, click on the *Add New Record* button at the top of the page. A new empty record will appear beneath the other (or others) for you to edit. Click again to add another. For now, however, return to your first entry.

5

You don't need to fill in all the boxes for each person. You can simply leave the box blank, if you prefer. If you have a picture or media file saved on your computer and you want to add it with a person's record, click the *Insert Media File* button next to that person's listing.

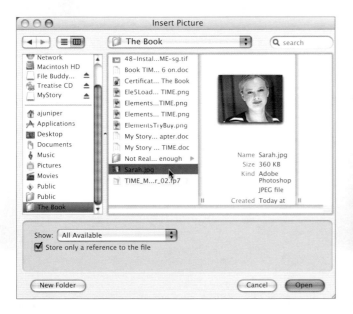

6

An *Insert...* box will appear, which allows you to locate the picture on your computer. This might look slightly different, depending on your operating system. Locate the picture and click *Open*.

7

The picture you choose will now appear in the box to the left of the list on the My Friends page.

Creating a list of your friends is useful, but it doesn't tell the whole story. That's why each friend also has an individual page for his or her picture, and space for related anecdotes.

1 Click on the *Enlarge Picture* icon next to the appropriate friend in the list view. You don't need to have a picture to do this.

2 You will see a page with the picture—if there is one—at full size, the nickname at the top right of the screen, and a space beneath it. This is where you can add as much text as you like about your friend.

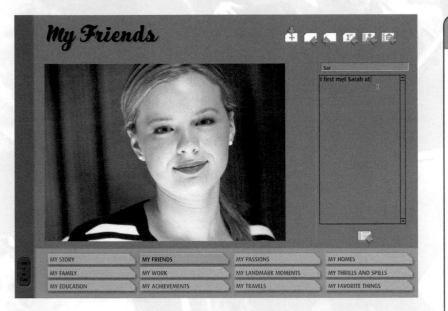

3 Click on the blank area and begin writing about your friend. What you say is your choice, but if you're stuck for ideas see "Writer's Block!" to the right.

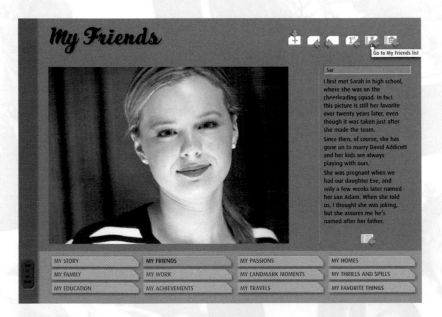

4 When you have finished, click the *Go to My Friends List* button to return to the list view. From there you can enter more friends.

✍ WRITER'S BLOCK!

Even if you've known your friends for a long time, it isn't always easy to know what to say about them. Here are some ideas to help you:

► Where or when did you first meet? Was it at school, in the office, or just last Thursday?

► What were you doing at the time? This may lead to an interesting anecdote.

► If you are writing about a long-time buddy from your local bar, why not add the bar to your My Places section, too?

► Mention some of the most memorable activities you've shared. A landmark birthday party or a fun vacation?

► Remember this is the story of your life, so be sure to include friends you no longer see, but who were an important part of your life.

► Were you and your spouse friends before you were partners? If so, why not include them here?

Adding more friends

If you've already used all of the blank friend slots that were initially provided, it's easy to add more as you need them.

An *Add New Record* button is located at the top of the My Friends list (and in the other sections of *My Story* where you can add more information).

1 Check for spare slots by scrolling to the bottom of the window.

2 Click the *Create a New Record in this Chapter* button at the top of the screen.

3 Enter your friend's information just as you did on page 58.

HELP DESK

You can also delete a record using the *Trash Can* icon to the right of its entry in the list. For more information, see page 94.

Finding friends

After a while you'll have a large collection of friends, and it might not always be easy to find a particular person. To make it easier to locate a certain friend, you can automatically organize your list in alphabetical order. You can even choose whether to sort by first or last name.

1 Move the mouse cursor to the top of the screen and click on the *Sort by First Name* button.

2 The list is now organized by first name. To help you keep organized, the record you edited most recently will be visible on the screen, even if it isn't at the top.

3 Click on the *Sort by Last Name* option to list your friends by last name instead. If any of your friends have the same last name, they will be organized alphabetically by first name within the surname group.

HELP DESK

If your list is longer than the six entries you can see on the screen, you can move up and down the list using the scroll bars and arrow buttons around the window, just as you would any other window on your computer. The toolbar and shortcuts will remain in place, but the rest of the list will scroll.

Your passions

Whether it's antiques or zoology, or anything in between, everyone's life is driven by their passions or hobbies, which is why this is a section of the book you'll keep coming back to time and time again.

If your life has led you in different directions, from a childhood fascination with steam trains to a youthful enthusiasm for the stars of the silver screen and a more mature interest in fine wines, then each of these topics should be separate chapters. The clever thing about this chapter is that it allows you to add as many subpages as you need.

1 Open the My Passions page from the *Main* menu, or use the shortcuts bar at the bottom of the page. You can add a new entry by clicking in an empty text box and typing.

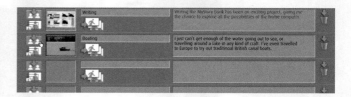

2 Next to your entry on the My Passions front page list, add your favorite photograph of that passion or hobby to accompany the section.

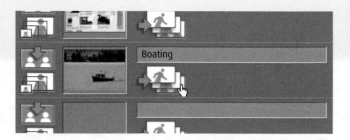

3 To add a little more depth to the entry, click on the *More About* button that appears beneath the passion's name.

4 You will find your favorite picture of your hobby at the top of a new almost blank list labeled "More about my passions." Start typing more detail about the picture you've added.

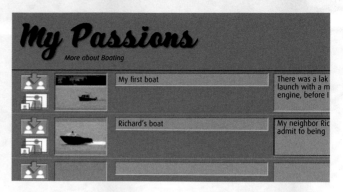

5 In the next record on the list, you can add another photo that represents a different aspect of your hobby, and write a caption about it.

6 Click on the *Enlarge Picture* icon next to a picture to see more details.

7 The *Enlarge Picture* screen lets you see the picture more clearly and write more in the caption. The text you write here also appears in the list view and vice versa.

📝 **WRITER'S BLOCK!**

Of course the word passions has another meaning, too. You can also think of this as a place to record the romances that have defined your life.

HELP DESK ▶

If you collect stamps, then scanning some of your favorites is a no-brainer. But don't forget that you can scan other small objects, too. Pick your favorite item from each category as the main image for that particular section.

Your homes

It's not until you think about it that you realize just how dramatic an influence on your life your homes have been. Where you live affects whom you meet, what schools you attend, and some of the language you use. Even if you choose to ignore the broad influences that a region has on you, every room of every home you've lived in is filled with memories—some funny, some sad— but all of them affect you in different ways.

HELP DESK

Faded photos of your first home are prime candidates for digital restoration. See Chapter 5 for more info.

For that reason, the My Homes page is structured just like the My Passions section (described on pages 64-65), with subpages to give you space for all of your stories, and accompanying pictures, in subchapters.

1 Open the My Homes list from the shortcuts bar or the *Main* menu page and add an address using the buttons and text boxes (see pages 64–65).

2 Click on the *More About* button next to the house to begin writing detailed stories about that particular home, rather than the basic address details.

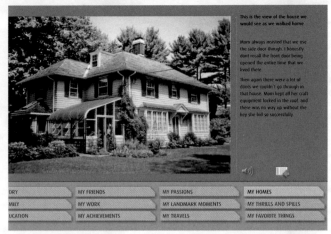

3 To add more text to the same photograph, click the *Enlarge Photo* button and continue typing in the larger text box. Use this space to expand your brief caption and describe your memories in more detail.

4 To return to the *More About* list, click on the button beneath the text area. This goes back one level to the list of pictures seen in step 2, while the similar icon on that page returns you to the view in step 1.

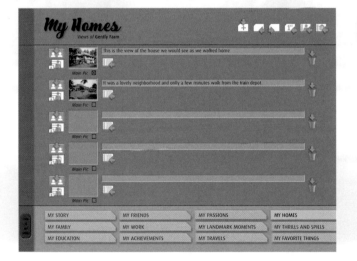

5 However, before you leave the specific home list (in step 2), you can also add additional photos of that home or something related to it. In this case, a picture from the neighborhood is added.

✍ **WRITER'S BLOCK!**

► Don't forget to mention when you moved into the home and when you left it.

► Did you have a favorite place in the home, or a tree house in the yard?

► Was there anything unusual about the home—an outside door that was very attractive or a screen door that people kept walking into?

► Remember to include pictures of favorite occasions within the home, and add some photos of the neighborhood.

Your place, from space

HELP DESK

A few faded old photographs might be enough to bring back memories of a former home, but if you want to capture a bit more about the neighborhood (or perhaps just get an unusual view), it might be worth trying out some of the exciting new tools that are available on the Internet.

Google Earth is a program that can be downloaded onto your computer (either a Mac or PC) and it allows you to zoom in on places around the globe, using satellite imagery to show a city, town, or even the street where you live.

Google Earth is a separate program which, although free, does not just work within an Internet browser. You must load it and install it onto your computer by taking the follwing steps:

1. Navigate your Internet browser to: http://earth.google.com

2. Choose the appropriate version for your computer (Mac or Windows) and begin the download.

3. When the program has finished downloading, it should install automatically. If not, double click on the file you downloaded to install it.

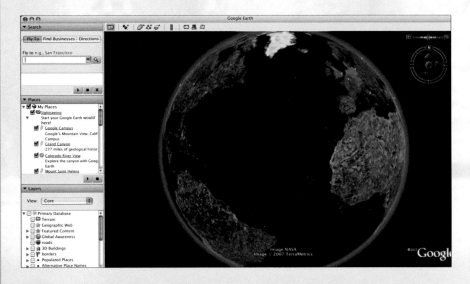

1 Make sure you are connected to the Internet, then open the Google Earth program. Initially you will see a view of the whole planet.

2 Type your address into the search field at the top left. If it is not inside the United States, add a comma and the name of the country, such as 12a Park Lane, London, United Kingdom.

3 Click the *OK* button and the Earth view will rotate and zoom in on the spot you have chosen.

4 When the program settles on one spot, you can use the compass symbol to zoom in and out by dragging the slider. You can also click-and-drag the satellite view to move left and right. As you navigate, detailed views are quickly loaded from the Internet.

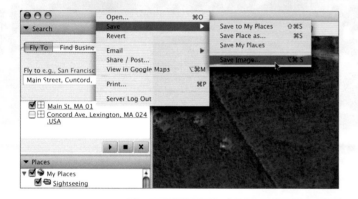

5 Click *File>Save>Save Image* to save your current view. You can use this picture as one of the views of your home.

6 If you want to track down a point of interest, try clicking on the *Places* icon to the left of the screen.

7 To be more specific, there are many subcategories within *Places*. Click the + icon to see them, and uncheck those that do not interest you. Nodes on the satellite view are only shown if their categories are checkmarked.

Your family

For most of us there will always be two tiers of family: the immediate family whom we live with every day and those aunts, uncles, cousins, and in-laws who are also a part of our lives. For that reason, the first screen you'll see when you open the My Family section is a simple choice between My Immediate Family and My Relatives. This makes it easier to reach the pages for your immediate family when you want to add an additional picture or comment. There is also an extensive range of possibilities within the My Relatives section.

It is up to you to decide which family members are immediate or relative, but it seems logical to think of your immediate family as the people at home with you.

FAMILY GROUPS

Immediate Family
• Wife
• Husband
• Partner
• Children
• Parents

Relatives
• Aunts and Uncles
• Mother and Father-in-Law
• Cousins
• Brothers and Sisters
  (if they live somewhere else)

WRITER'S BLOCK!

► If you're writing about your children, remember that people are usually interested in how much they weighed when they were born and any other interesting stories.

► What was your child's first word?

► How did you meet your wife? Did she say yes the first time you asked her out on a date?

► Was there anything you did that really annoyed your parents?

► Try and find some pictures that show your family members at different ages.

 Select either My Immediate Family or My Relatives.

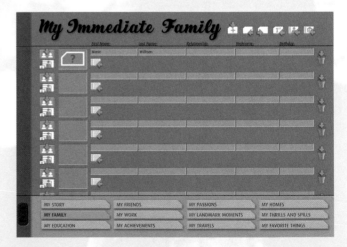

2 In the list view that follows, click on a blank field and add the name of a family member.

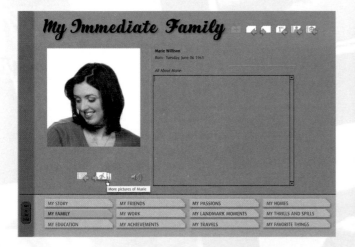

3 The third column, "Relationship," lets you describe how the person is related to you. A list of choices is provided, which you can see by clicking on the field. To choose one, click on it. If you prefer to write your own, you may still do this by typing directly into the field. Now add a picture using the *Insert Media* button (see page 56).

4 The picture will appear in the thumbnail. You can also add the person's birthday by using a drop-down menu. Click once in the *Birthday* box and a small *Calendar* button appears at the right end of the dialog box. Click on this to open a calendar. Simply click on the up/down arrows to select the year and the left/right ones until the correct month is displayed, then pick the day.

5 There is a *More About* button beneath the *Insert Media* button. Click on it to bring up a window with a larger copy of the picture you added and a large caption box. Next, click on the *More Pictures* button.

6 The *More Pictures* button in the detail page takes you to a list page that has unlimited space for you to add pictures of your family member. Each of these can be viewed at a large size using the *Detail* button.

Your work

Chances are you've spent a good portion of your life at work. Work is both an important part of who we are and—from a historical perspective—it tells potential readers a great deal about our current society. It's understandable if you don't want to dwell on the hours you have spent making money for somebody else, but you cannot record a complete life picture without including something about your work. On the other hand, if you're a self-made millionaire, you may enjoy filling in this section!

Whatever you do to earn a living, there are usually memorable events along the way. Did you have a paper route, or a lemonade stand when you were a kid? Even the most humdrum employment usually begins with a nerve-tingling interview. How was yours? But before we get to that topic it's a good idea to start off with the employer's name.

1 Begin by clicking in the text boxes and typing in the company name and location. You will be able to add separate job roles when you get to step 4.

2 In the *Date Started* and *Until* boxes, click once to reveal the *Calendar* button, then click on it to open the calendar (as described on page 71).

3 To add a picture, right click on the picture box and choose *Insert Media*. After following the insert picture steps (see page 56), click the *More About* button.

4 In the page that appears, you can add any anecdotes about your job into the large caption box. You can also add your job title or titles in the column to the left.

5 Afterward you can either return to the previous page to add more past and current jobs, or use the *More About* button to add extra pictures of the job.

WRITER'S BLOCK!

► What did the company do?

► What was your boss like?

► What were your best moments—the biggest deals, best products made, or simply the most enjoyable part of the job?

► Who were your co-workers?

► How and why did you leave?

Landmark moments

If you picture the route your life has taken, it is probably not a straight line, but a path that has switched directions at several stages. Even if you followed a plan from your childhood, you probably needed to take some breaks along the way.

These points are the landmark moments in your life, and it's often interesting to look back on them and see what they meant to you. If you were writing a traditional autobiography, these subjects would probably need chapters of their own.

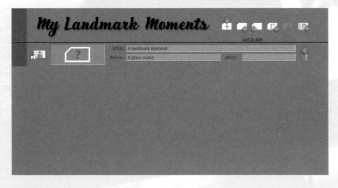

1 Switch to the My Landmark Moments page from the shortcuts bar at the bottom of the page or from the front page.

2 Type your caption into the text box, then click the *More About* button to the left.

3 Click the *Detail* button to the left of the landmark moment you've just described. You will be taken to a new list view with a blank entry. Import a media file using the *Add Media File* button to the left, then type a caption into the space.

4 Click on the *Detail* button for the record to see a large version of the file and add a longer caption.

My Landmark Moments
Deciding to change my major

I was gazing up at the clock tower when I made my decision

Main Pic ☒

The books that held no interest for me

Main Pic ☐

My designer's pencils

Main Pic ☐

A designer's computer

Main Pic ☐

My Studio

MY STORY	MY FRIENDS	MY PASSIONS	MY HOMES
MY FAMILY	MY WORK	MY LANDMARK MOMENTS	MY THRILLS AND SPILLS
MY EDUCATION	MY ACHIEVEMENTS	MY TRAVELS	MY FAVORITE THINGS

My Landmark Moments
Deciding to change my major

Main Pic ☐

The books that held no interest for me

Main Pic

My designer's pencils

Main Pic

A designer's computer

Main Pic

My Studio

Main Pic

MY STORY	MY FRIENDS	MY PASSIONS	MY HOMES
MY FAMILY	MY WORK	MY LANDMARK MOMENTS	MY THRILLS AND SPILLS
MY EDUCATION	MY ACHIEVEMENTS	MY TRAVELS	MY FAVORITE THINGS

5 When you have finished describing your landmark moment, click on the *Return to List* button beneath the caption you wrote. Use the list view to add any other media files relevant to that landmark moment.

6 If you would like to use another media file to represent the landmark moment in the main Landmark Moments page (seen in step one), check the *Main Pic* box beneath your chosen file.

WRITER'S BLOCK!

► If you went to college, how did you decide on your major? If you switched majors, this counts as a separate milestone.

► Did you decide to follow a family business or switch from it?

► Did something happen to change your life—even if you had no control over it?

► What first attracted you to your chosen career? If you chose acting, was it your first school play?

► Where did you propose and when were you married?

My Landmark Moments
Sort by date

| What: | Deciding to change my major | | |
| Where: | College | When: | |

| What: | The first time I saw a Pontiac Firebird | | |
| Where: | My uncle's house | When: | 05/05/1968 |

MY STORY	MY FRIENDS	MY PASSIONS	MY HOMES
MY FAMILY	MY WORK	MY LANDMARK MOMENTS	MY THRILLS AND SPILLS
MY EDUCATION	MY ACHIEVEMENTS	MY TRAVELS	MY FAVORITE THINGS

7 When you press the *Back* button to return to the main Landmark Moments page, you will see the thumbnail representing the moment has been replaced with the one you chose in step six. You can now continue to add more landmark moments.

Thrills and spills

While the landmark moments on the previous pages have metaphorically propelled you in one direction or another, what about those occasions when you've literally been thrown around? What really excites you? Do you seek out the highest roller coasters, climb the highest mountains, or ski down them as rapidly as possible?

This is the section to record all the activities that make your blood pump faster and your adrenalin flow. Don't worry, there's plenty of space for media files!

HELP DESK

There is no need to add everything in the order it happened. At any point you can click the *Sort By Date* button at the top of the list. The program will do the work for you.

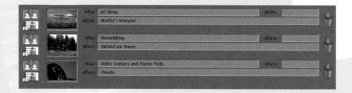

1 The main Thrills and Spills view is a simple list view with one text box, a date box, and a media box.

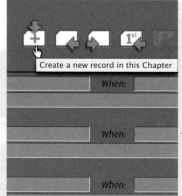

2 To add a new record, click the *New Record* button (at the left end of the tool strip at the top of the screen).

✎ WRITER'S BLOCK!

► Have you ever been white-water rafting or do you enjoy any kind of adventurous activity?

► Have you learned to fly?

► Do you have any photos of you taking part in the activity?

► You can add as many excursions as you like, so why not use this opportunity to show how your skills have developed or how the challenge has increased over time?

3 Begin to add your record. If you want to add a movie, click on the *Insert Media* button and choose *Insert Video,* rather than the *Picture* option.

4 Use the window that appears to locate the movie clip you prepared earlier. This window is generated by your computer's operating system, so it might look slightly different, but it will work the same way. For more on preparing movie clips, see pages 36 and 148.

5 The movie will be copied into a special *My Story* folder on your hard drive as described in the box on page 48 (Windows) or page 51 (Mac). A movie icon will appear in the thumbnail box. You can view the movie and add a full-length caption from the detail page by clicking the *Detail View* button next to the *Movie* icon.

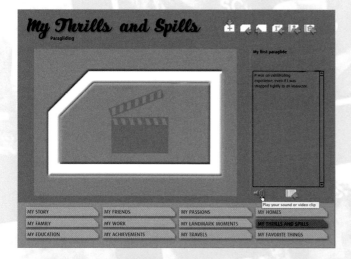

6 You can use the larger view to add a more detailed caption to explain the movie clip. When you are finished, click the *Play* button to play the video clip.

7 A timeline with simple controls will appear. You can click the *Play/Pause* button in the bottom left to pause or resume playback at any point.

Your education

Because it is divided into two pages, filling in the My Education section is a breeze. The first page is a simple screen that allows you to select your different levels of education—school or college.

This section is designed to allow you to add several media files from each of the schools you attended using a list view, detail view, and a thumbnail page. This final page allows you to add up to six media files and still see large clear thumbnails. You can click also though to a larger view.

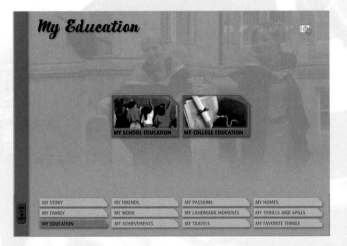

1 From the first page you can click on the relevant button to go to the appropriate page. There is room for you to add the name of the school and the years you attended it.

2 Using the list view, add the schools you have attended and your favorite picture of each one by using the *Add Media* button to the left of the entry. Afterward, click the *Detail* button.

WRITER'S BLOCK!

► Who was your best friend at school?

► What was your most embarrassing moment?

► What were your school's colors?

► Who were your most influential teachers?

3 The My School Education detail page allows you to add your thoughts on the school, as well as the names of the teachers and students you remember. It's a good idea to press Return to add a new line after each name.

4 Click on the *Detail* button in each school's detail page to see this special media page. You can add up to six media items related to the school.

5 Fill the page with as many pictures as you wish. Why not scan some from your yearbook, if you have one?

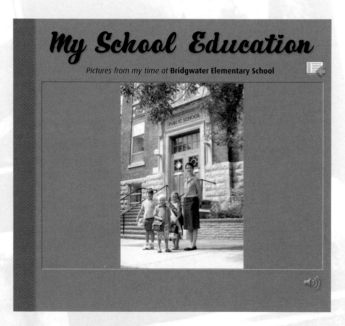

6 For a closer look at any of the media files, simply click the *Detail* button next to each image and a separate window will appear. Close this window when you are done.

Your achievements

HELP DESK

If you have a certificate, why not scan it in and put it in the media box? You can improve the quality of a scan by following the advice on page 146.

Whether it's graduating from high school or sailing around the world, everyone has special moments to be proud of. This section is a place to record yours, and perhaps illustrate them with video clips or a diploma or certificate.

Any goal that you set and met or any hurdle that you've overcome is an achievement worth including. Have you raised money for a charity or were you awarded an academic achievement? The great thing about achievements is that they're yours to define. You can restrict yourself to more formal qualifications or expand your page to include sports championships, classes you've taught, and more.

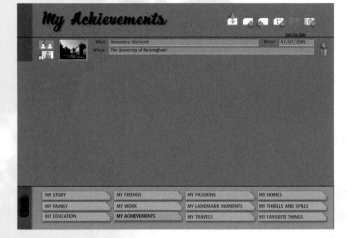

1 Open the My Achievements page. You'll find it is similar to the Thrills and Spills section. It has a clean layout with a text box, a date box, and a media frame for each item in the list.

2 Describe your achievement and what it meant to you in the larger view accessed via the *More About* button. If you haven't added a photo or media file, you will need to go back to the list view.

My Achievements

Sort by date

| What: | Honorary Doctorate | When: | 07/07/2005 |
| Where: | The University of Birmingham | | |

| What: | Teaching my daughter to drive | When: | |
| Where: | | | |

| What: | Black-and-White photography Course | When: | |
| Where: | Local college | | |

| What: | Winning the local league with my office soccer team | When: | |
| Where: | G. E. Neric Holdings, Inc. | | |

| What: | Won 2nd Prize in the flower show | When: | |
| Where: | Concord, MA | | |

| What: | Management Training Course | When: | |
| Where: | City Academy, Boston, MA | | |

| What: | | When: | |

MY STORY MY FRIENDS MY PASSIONS MY HOMES

MY FAMILY MY WORK MY LANDMARK MOMENTS MY THRILLS AND SPILLS

MY EDUCATION MY ACHIEVEMENTS MY TRAVELS MY FAVORITE THINGS

► Do you have a professional certification? Why not scan the certificate?

► Don't worry about poking a little fun at yourself. If you ever came in last in a competition, why not mention that?

► Achievements don't have to be academic or sports related. What about karaoke?

► Consider some very personal achievements, too. For example, have you ever helped someone improve himself?

► How did the achievement make you feel?

Your travels

Whether by land, sea, or air, travel broadens the mind. Take some time to collect your favorite vacation photos and home movies to add to your My Travels section. It would be a shame not to include them!

The My Travels section, like the preceding *My Story* pages, expands to allow you as much space as you need to include every expedition you've ever taken and every picture, video, or scrap of information you can find from the trip. To streamline the page's appearance, you can start with your favorite picture.

✍ WRITER'S BLOCK!

► Where have you traveled while serving your country or your employer?

► Try and remember all your vacations as far back as you can.

► How did you travel? Did you drive a long distance?

► Remember that you can scan old postcards and other mementos, too.

► You don't need to limit this page to vacations abroad; any memorable trip can fit in this section.

► Don't forget to include your honeymoon!

My Travels

	My trip to:	The beach
	The purpose:	Vacation
	My trip to:	The beach
	The purpose:	Vacation
	My trip to:	The mountains
	The purpose:	Educational
	My trip to:	Rome
	The purpose:	Business
	My trip to:	Venice
	The purpose:	Conference
	My trip to:	New York in Winter
	The purpose:	Vacation
	My trip to:	

MY STORY   MY FRIENDS   MY PASSIONS

11/15/2004	11/26/2004
11/20/2007	11/21/2007
11/22/2007	11/23/2007
01/07/2007	01/10/2007

◀   January 2008   ▲▼ ▶

Mon	Tue	Wed	Thu	Fri	Sat	Sun
31	1	2	3	4	5	6
7	8	9	10	11	12	13
14	15	16	17	18	19	20
21	22	23	24	25	26	27
28	29	30	31	1	2	3
4	5	6	7	8	9	10

Today: 11/20/2007

MY PASSIONS

MY LANDMARK MOMENTS

MY TRAVELS

---

1 Open the My Travels section and fill in an entry with the location of a trip. If the trip was special in some way—to see the fall leaves in New England or a family reunion—there is room to include that detail in the title.

2 To save your typing fingers, use the drop-down *Purpose* menu to specify the reason for your trip. Simply click on the text box for a list of options. You can also use automatic date-entry tools.

My Travels

Rome
Business

All about my trip to Rome:
It's very hard to remember the exact details of my time at school, but in my memory so much more time was spent outdoors than in a classroom. that cannot really be true, but there were a lot of enjoyable school trips, and even the dinners tasted. If only I'd been any good in the school play.

Who came with me on the trip to Rome:

I was travelling alone

Places I visited on this trip to Rome:

The Flavian Ampitheatre (better known as "The Colosseum")
The Spanish Steps
The Olympic Stadium

MY STORY	MY FRIENDS	MY PASSIONS	MY HOMES
MY FAMILY	MY WORK	MY LANDMARK MOMENTS	MY THRILLS AND SPILLS
MY EDUCATION	MY ACHIEVEMENTS	MY TRAVELS	MY FAVORITE THINGS

My Travels
My trip to **Rome**

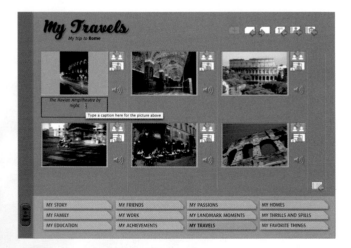

The Flavian Ampitheatre by night

Type a caption here for the picture above

MY STORY	MY FRIENDS	MY PASSIONS	MY HOMES
MY FAMILY	MY WORK	MY LANDMARK MOMENTS	MY THRILLS AND SPILLS
MY EDUCATION	MY ACHIEVEMENTS	MY TRAVELS	MY FAVORITE THINGS

---

3 In the list view, click on the empty media box to add a picture or a movie that summarizes the trip, then click on the *Detail* view button to bring up a page where you can add a full description of your trip.

4 There is another detail view—accessed by the button in the lower left of the previous screen, beneath the media window. This page allows you to add additional media files and captions.

Your favorite things

This part of *My Story* does not just cover material possessions, although there is ample room for everything you have or could ever desire. Instead, this section provides you with the chance to explore every facet of your personality, whether it is the music you love, the films you watch, or the time in history that most fascinates you. If you think this is a lot of information, you're right. The My Favorite Things section is so big that it has another 12 menu buttons that are similar to the main home page.

The best way to explore this section is to simply start using it. In this example, you'll see how the information you enter into the list field affects what appears beneath in the detail view. This acts the same way as other sections of *My Story*, but it is especially useful in this section.

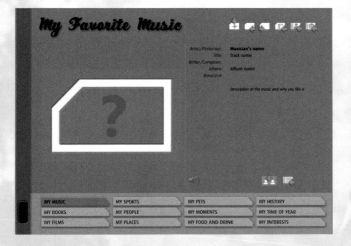

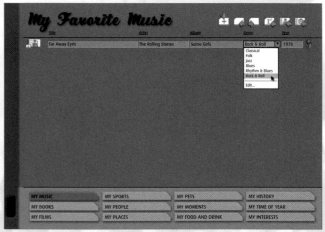

1 Open the Music page and, if you immediately click on the detail view with the button to the left, you'll find a blank page. Don't edit this page yet, but click back with the *Previous Page* button (second from the right in the *Toolbar*).

2 Now enter the information about the favorite song you want to include. You can include as many songs as you wish by pressing the *New Record* button, but just add one for now.

My Favorite Books

1984
by George Orwell

My rating: ★★★★★

Why I like this book:

Published in 1948, this book remains disturbingly prescient in many respects. It tells the story of party worker Winston Smith, in a totalitarian society run by "Big Brother," as he tries and ultimately fails to disrupt the government.

The story begins "as the clocks were striking 13," and that is far from the only striking thought contained within the relatively modest length. The thought of perpetual war to keep the Proles distracted, and the idea of the Ministry of Truth actualy removing words from the language to create "Newspeak" (a language in which it is impossible to express discontent) are just some of the ideas that stick in the mind.

Not to mention Room 101.

About the author

George Orwell was in fact the pen name of George Arthur Blair, born in 1903 in British India. Soon after a commission to write about the underprivledged George travelled to spain to fight against Fascist General Franco. Not only did he write about his experiences there, but went on - via the BBC where he had to work with the UK's Ministry of Information during the war - to write Animal Farm and 1984. He died of TB in 1950.

Published 1948
by Penguin

MY MUSIC	MY SPORTS	MY PETS	MY HISTORY
MY BOOKS	MY PEOPLE	MY MOMENTS	MY TIME OF YEAR
MY FILMS	MY PLACES	MY FOOD AND DRINK	MY INTERESTS

Back to previous page button

Each detail page within My Favorite Things has been designed for the subject matter. In the My Favorite Books page, you can say why you like both the book and the author.

My Favorite Music

Artist/Performer: **The Rolling Stones**
Title: Far Away Eyes
Writer/Composer: Mick Jagger (arguably)
Album: Some Girls
Recorded: 1978

The Rolling Stone's answer to the Punk movement which had sprung up in the time they had been on the scene.

MY MUSIC	MY SPORTS	MY PETS	MY HISTORY
MY BOOKS	MY PEOPLE	MY MOMENTS	MY TIME OF YEAR
MY FILMS	MY PLACES	MY FOOD AND DRINK	MY INTERESTS

My Favorite Season

A crisp New England winter's day

Winter

My favorite time of year is winter, because I love those occasional days with crisp, clear sun brightening a cold start. I also love spending this holiday season with my family.

MY MUSIC	MY SPORTS	MY PETS	MY HISTORY
MY BOOKS	MY PEOPLE	MY MOMENTS	MY TIME OF YEAR
MY FILMS	MY PLACES	MY FOOD AND DRINK	MY INTERESTS

3 When you have entered the information, click the *Detail* button again and you'll see that some of the boxes have been filled in with the information you provided on the previous page. Add the remaining details and any media files that remind you of the music.

The My Favorite Season page gives you the chance to add a single picture to represent your favorite time of the year. You can use the caption box to explain why you enjoy the time of year so much and describe your media file, too.

Adding more favorites

There's often a lot to say about something you really enjoy. Because each section within your favorites has been tailored to its specific area, it has detail pages specially designed for the type of material you will be entering. The steps on this page will show you exactly how to complete a specialized section.

For example, why not add one of your favorite movies to the *My Story* program? In this case, we'll be starting from an empty list and adding the first entry, but you can add as many entries as you like by using the *Add New Record* button at the top of the page. There is no limit to the number of films you can add to the list, so why not mention your entire movie collection?

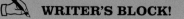

WRITER'S BLOCK!

► Are you writing about your favorite movie but can't remember some of the details? If you have access to the Internet, visit the Internet Movie Database (www.imdb.com), which works like a search engine just for films. You'll find all you need to know about any film you can recall.

1 Open the My Favorites page and go to the Films section by clicking on the button in the lower left corner of the page. Notice that the only *Toolbar* button available at the top returns you to the Home page. There aren't any areas on this page that you can edit; instead, you must choose one of the 12 subcategories to work on.

2 The *Film* menu allows you to enter a large number of films and see them in a list view. Remember, this is simply meant to be a list of films that are important to you, so don't worry whether you saw it at the cinema, own the DVD, or have seen it on television. Click in each field from left to right and type in the details of the film.

Edit Value List "Film Genre"

Romance
Romantic comedy
Sci-Fi
Thriller
Western
Adventure

_

Cancel   OK

3 To add a genre, click on the *Genre* field and a drop-down arrow will appear on the right. Click on it for a list of options or, if you don't see the one you want, choose the *Edit* option.

4 If you choose to edit the field, you'll see a list of genres. Click after the last genre and press Return to insert a new line. Type the name of your new genre and click OK.

5 You can now click on the field again to open the drop-down menu and choose your new category by clicking on it.

6 The far right box allows you to rate the movie, from one to five stars. Perhaps you're going to give every movie five stars, but it might be just as interesting to record the movies you do not like for posterity. To explain your thoughts more, click on the *Detail* button at the left.

7 The Detail button opens a new page that has room to add a media file—perhaps a film poster, or a clip from the movie—cast names, a full review, and a plot summary. When you have finished, simply click on the *Back* button (in the lower left of the screen) to return to the *Films* list.

Sorting your favorites

From childhood onward most of us have created lists of our favorite things, discussing with friends the various reasons why a book or movie is considered the greatest of all time. These debates can persist indefinitely, but the *My Story* program will enable you to put the arguments aside and rate things your way.

A nice feature of *My Story* is you don't have to include anything you don't want on your pages. And there is the rating tool introduced on page 87, which you can use to indicate your favorites. But you can also sort by rating, too. For example, you'll be able to quickly find your all-time favorite books. Better still, you are not restricted to a clumsy "top 10"—you are able to see all of your five-star favorites, followed by others that do not rate as high.

Another advantage of this approach is that it works naturally with the other sorting tools provided in *My Story*, so you will have no trouble remembering how to sort by book title or author name, too. With the methods described on this page, you'll be able to keep all your books—or films, music, or other favorites—arranged however you like, using just a single click.

1 As you can see, a long list of books might make it hard to instantly find your favorites. Luckily they have all been assigned star ratings.

2 If you see a star rating that you disagree with— perhaps you've recently re-read the book or had time to reflect on its message—then simply click on it and choose a new rating from the pop-up list.

My Favorite Books

Title:	Author First Name:	Author Last Name:	Publisher:	Pub:	Rating:
1984	George	Orwell	Penguin	1948	*****
Pride and Prejudice	Jane	Austen	Penguin	1813	****
I know Why the Caged Bird Sings	Maya	Angelou	Bantam	1969	*****
To Kill a Mocking Bird	Harper	Lee	Harper Collins	1960	****
Frankenstein	Mary	Shelley	Lackington, Hughes	1818	***
Casino Royale	Ian	Flemming	Jonathan Cape	1953	****
Of Mice and Men	John	Steinbeck	Spangler	1937	***
The Grapes of Wrath	John	Steinbeck	Viking Press	1939	****
Do Androids Dream of Electric Sheep	Phillip K.	Dick	Doubleday	1968	***
Adventures of Huckleberry Finn	Mark	Twain	Webster	1884	****
Catcher in the Rye	J.D.	Salinger	Little, Brown & Co	1951	*

MY MUSIC · MY SPORTS · MY PETS · MY HISTORY
MY BOOKS · MY PEOPLE · MY MOMENTS · MY TIME OF YEAR
MY FILMS · MY PLACES · MY FOOD AND DRINK · MY INTERESTS

My Favorite Books

Title:	Author First Name:	Author Last Name:	Publisher:	Pub:	Rating:
1984	George	Orwell	Penguin	1948	***
Adventures of Huckleberry Finn	Mark	Twain	Webster	1884	***
Casino Royale	Ian	Flemming	Jonathan Cape	1953	***
Catcher in the Rye	J.D.	Salinger	Little, Brown & Co	1951	*
Do Androids Dream of Electric Sheep	Phillip K.	Dick	Doubleday	1968	***
Frankenstein	Mary	Shelley	Lackington, Hughes	1818	***
I know Why the Caged Bird Sings	Maya	Angelou	Bantam	1969	*****
Of Mice and Men	John	Steinbeck	Spangler	1937	***
Pride and Prejudice	Jane	Austen	Penguin	1813	****
The Grapes of Wrath	John	Steinbeck	Viking Press	1939	***
To Kill a Mocking Bird	Harper	Lee	Harper Collins	1960	****

MY MUSIC · MY SPORTS · MY PETS · MY HISTORY
MY BOOKS · MY PEOPLE · MY MOMENTS · MY TIME OF YEAR
MY FILMS · MY PLACES · MY FOOD AND DRINK · MY INTERESTS

3 Now click the underlined word "Ratings" at the top of the column and all of the records will be arranged in the order of the number of stars you have awarded them. To see the lower-ranked items, scroll down using the *Next Record* button or the scroll bar at the side of the window.

4 In this case, the books have been sorted by title simply by clicking on the word "Title" at the top of the page. You might prefer to leave your records sorted this way rather than by rating—the choice is yours.

SORTING BY ALPHABET

Of course, you aren't restricted to using the sort function for ranking your favorites. You'll notice that all of the category headings in the sections of *My Story* are also underlined. This allows you to click on them to sort the records in order based on the column beneath. If it is a text column, such as author names, it will be sorted alphabetically. If the information is numerical, it will be arranged numerically. In the case of a combination, numbers will appear before letters. Dates are arranged in chronological order.

My Favorite Books

Title:	Author First Name:	Author Last Name:	Publisher:	Pub:	Rating:
I know Why the Caged Bird Sings	Maya	Angelou	Bantam	1969	*****
Pride and Prejudice	Jane	Austen	Penguin	1813	****
Do Androids Dream of Electric Sheep	Phillip K.	Dick	Doubleday	1968	***
Casino Royale	Ian	Flemming	Jonathan Cape	1953	****
Too Kill a Mocking Bird	Harper	Lee	Harper Collins	1960	****
1984	George	Orwell	Penguin	1948	*****
Catcher in the Rye	J.D.	Salinger	Little, Brown & Co	1951	*
Frankenstein	Mary	Shelley	Lackington, Hughes	1818	***
Of Mice and Men	John	Steinbeck	Spangler	1937	***
The Grapes of Wrath	John	Steinbeck	Viking Press	1939	****
Adventures of Huckleberry Finn	Mark	Twain	Webster	1884	****

MY MUSIC · MY SPORTS · MY PETS · MY HISTORY
MY BOOKS · MY PEOPLE · MY MOMENTS · MY TIME OF YEAR
MY FILMS · MY PLACES · MY FOOD AND DRINK · MY INTERESTS

Photographing objects

A collection of favorite things is easy to display in your home, but there's also a simple way to include these items in your story: Use a digital camera. Photographing an entire collection and copying the pictures into *My Story* costs you nothing except your time—and not very much of it!

Taking good photographs of individual collectibles is, like so much in photography, all about lighting. For most subjects you'll find that diffuse lighting—light that comes from many angles—produces the best results because all of the surfaces are lit. If you place the main light source to one side, you will usually find the opposite side of your object in shadow. However, light direct from the camera flash can have a very bleaching effect because it removes any sense of form. The ideal solution is to place the camera on a tripod and use available light, such as a window.

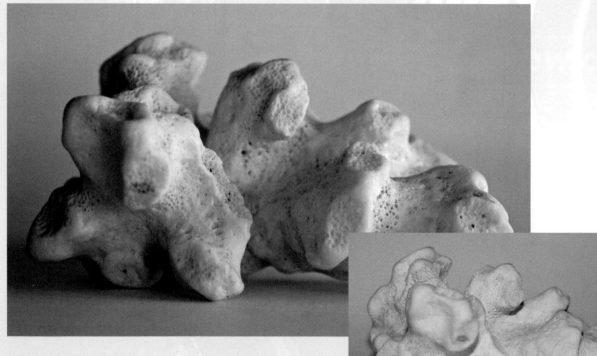

Flash and natural light
These are two images of the same subject. The left photo uses diffused lighting from the side and the right photo was taken with direct flash. It is clear which one looks the best.

1 Place your camera on a tripod or another supporting surface and arrange your subject in front of a plain background with a north-facing window or other diffuse light source nearby. If you're outside, clouds are a good source of diffused light.

2 Use the camera settings to disable the flash. The camera will be forced to set a longer shutter speed, which uses the natural light in your scene rather than the harsh flash.

3 Turn on the self-timer (the one you use to appear in your own photos).

4 Make sure that your camera can focus on the object—most lenses have a minimum focus distance so your object must be further away than this distance. Press the shutter and wait for the camera to capture your object.

5 Check the result, replace the object, and continue shooting. Unless they're especially large, it's usually easier to move the objects than the camera. In a sense, you've created a mini photography studio.

Light tent
A solution for serious and enthusiast photographers is a light tent. This is a thin fabric enclosure with a slot for the camera lens. An off-camera flash is fired outside the tent and the light is diffused by the material.

Mini-tripod
If you're using a digital compact model, you can pick up an inexpensive tripod at any camera store. If you're shooting small objects, this may be all you need.

HELP DESK

If you're shooting photographs—especially against a very light or dark background—make sure that the subject dominates the frame.

Most cameras use "center weighted metering," which means they set their exposure so the center of the shot looks the best in the final image.

If most of the center space is taken up by the background, the background may end up looking better than the main subject.

Editing text

As you build your narrative, you might decide that you want to change some previous entries. Perhaps you've made a simple spelling error or maybe one of your friends has reminded you about something you forgot.

Whatever the reason, you don't have to delete an entry and start again. *My Story* allows you to make changes whenever you want by browsing to the page you want to change and clicking in the part you want to edit.

These changes replace the original text automatically, without the need to manually press *Save*. The only hazard is that you may replace the wrong information, so remember to check where you are clicking.

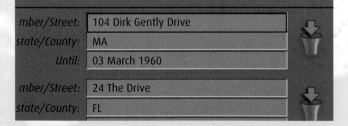

1 Imagine, for example, that you clicked on the *My Homes* button to add a new picture, but you noticed that your second home has the wrong address.

2 Click on the incorrect address at the point of the error. In this case, the correct address is 1024, so click immediately after the number you will delete.

3 Notice that the box has an outline and a flashing cursor has appeared, just as it did when you were entering text the first time. Use the Cursor keys to reposition the cursor if you missed the exact spot, then use the Backspace key to delete the mistake.

CUTTING LONGER MISTAKES

If you want to delete more than just a few characters, it is easier to select the text as a complete section. When you select text, it appears highlighted. When you begin to type, the text will be automatically replaced.

If you're fast on your fingers, you can double, triple, or quadruple click to select text. Alternatively, you can click and drag a section of text to highlight it.

The view of the house we saw every day as we walked up the drive.

Mom always insisted that we use the side door though. In all the years I lived there I don't recall that central door being opened.

Double click on a word to select it.

The view of the house we saw every day as we walked up the drive.

Mom always insisted that we use the side door though. In all the years I lived there I don't recall that central door being opened.

Triple click to select a whole line of text.

The view of the house we saw every day as we walked up the drive.

Mom always insisted that we use the side door though. In all the years I lived there I don't recall that central door being opened.

Quadruple click to select a whole paragraph.

4 Type your correction, then click somewhere outside the box so it ceases to be active. The black outline will disappear and the keyboard is no longer directly connected to the text box.

Replacing media

There may be times when you want to replace a photograph or delete an entry from *My Story*. Maybe you edited a picture in Photoshop or you've upgraded your camera equipment and want to replace your earlier snapshots with better pictures. Whatever the reason, it's easy to replace your images or completely remove an entry.

Building your life history in *My Story* is a task that is never quite complete because you live a little more each day. The *Add Media* button continues to welcome all compatible media types, even after you've added one. The first rule of replacement is that you can always go over a previous media file and replace it without the rips or tears you'd risk in a physical album.

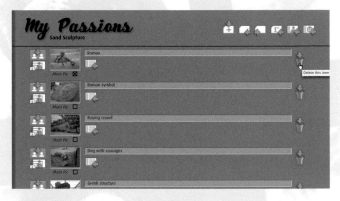

Deleting an individual image
To delete an individual image within a chapter, browse to the image in the chapter list. Select the individual image, and click on the *Trash Can* icon.

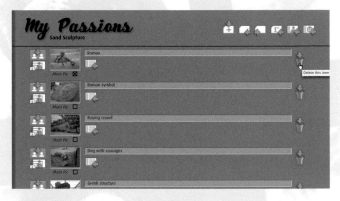

Deleting a whole chapter
To delete a whole chapter, locate it in the main list (such as the main My Passions page) and click on the *Trash Can* icon to the right of the chapter.

SECONDARY IMAGES

Instead of replacing an image, you can also swap it for another, so a different picture will appear at the top of the chapter:

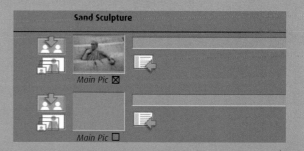

Because:

Passion: Sand sculpture

Because:

1. Click the *More About* button to view the contents of the chapter.

Sand Sculpture

Main Pic ☒

Main Pic ☐

2. Add your new image as a new record within the chapter. Add a caption if you wish.

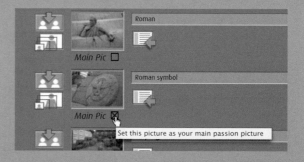

Roman

Main Pic ☐

Roman symbol

Main Pic ☒

Set this picture as your main passion picture

3. Click the *Main Pic* button. This image will become the icon image for this chapter on the main page.

○ ○ ○ Insert Media

What would you like to import?

Picture

Click to add a picture, sound or video clip

Video

100 ▭ ▤ ▥ Browse

Replacing an image
To replace an image, but keep the same caption, click on the image and then the *Insert Media* button to the left.

Creating a backup

Keeping a backup of all your work is sensible and very straightforward. If you have a vision of expensive and time-consuming tapes and dingy server rooms—put that thought away! The techniques here are simple and inexpensive.

The most practical way to keep a backup these days is on an external hard drive. These convenient devices can store many gigabytes of data and can be easily carried to another location. While you don't want to imagine the

worst happening, keeping your backup and your original data in different locations eliminates the risk of both items being lost at once.

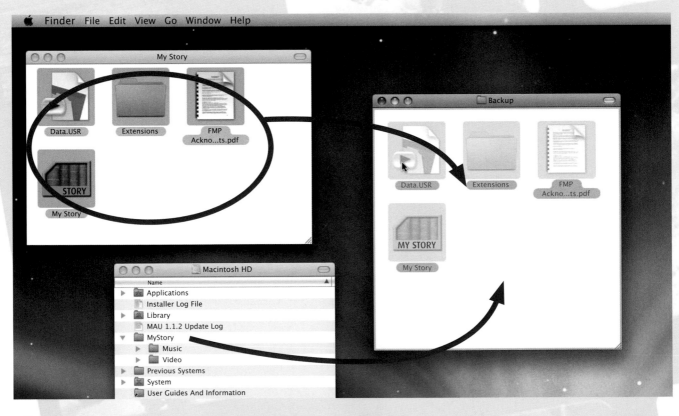

1 Be sure to close *My Story*. It's important to make sure you are not using the program when you create a duplicate of it.

2 Open the *Explorer* (PC) or *Finder* (Mac) window that contains the program and support files. Do not use a link or alias that you may have created (see page 52).

Open the *Explorer* or *Finder* window for your backup location. This must be on a different physical component—whether it's an external drive or on another part of your home network. Otherwise your computer will simply move the file.

 Drag the file you've been using to the external location and the computer will make a copy of it onto the new device.

5 Periodically reconnect to the external drive and copy the file to back it up.

HELP DESK

An increasingly popular solution to backing up your most important files is to use an online service. These services use extremely fast broadband connections to back up your important files to a computer that might be thousands of miles away.

AUTOMATED BACKUP

Another alternative is to use automated backup software, such as the software included with some versions of Windows Vista or with all Macintosh computers since OS X 10.5. These utilities can be configured to make automatic backups, and they also use easy-to-understand menus to help you restore any information when necessary. You'll just need to make sure that your *My Story* folder is part of your automatic backup:

1. Press the *Start* button and open the *Control Panel*.

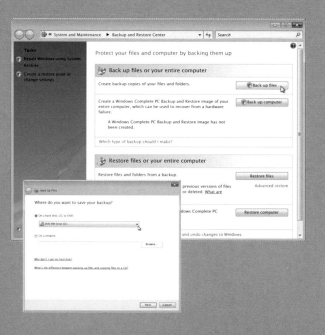

2. Locate the Backup and Restore Center (the Mac OS X equivalent is called Time Machine).

3. Follow the steps under *Backup Files* to make a backup. The computer will list all of the usable devices connected to the computer.

4

Sharing your story

After working for hours on your story, it would be a shame to hide it in your computer. In this connected age, there are many ways to share your creative work, whether you want to share one picture or every page.

In this chapter we explore: burning your *My Story* database onto a CD or DVD that can be read by other computers, printing out pages from the database, viewing your photos as a slideshow, and even copying your material into a blog to share with the world. That's a lot of possibilities. But most importantly, don't forget the simple pleasure of browsing through the pages on your own or showing them to your family.

Creating a CD

My *Story* is designed to work directly from the disc that it is stored on, which means that you can save or burn a copy onto a blank CD. You will not be able to edit the file on a CD, but you will be able to view it on other computers and copy it from the CD onto other machines.

My Story works best from a computer's internal hard drive because it can transfer data to and from the computer far more quickly than a CD. Therefore, if possible, it is a good idea to copy the database onto your computer

before you start to work on it (see page 48). It is important, when copying an edited version of *My Story*, to make sure that the file is closed so you cannot make changes by accident.

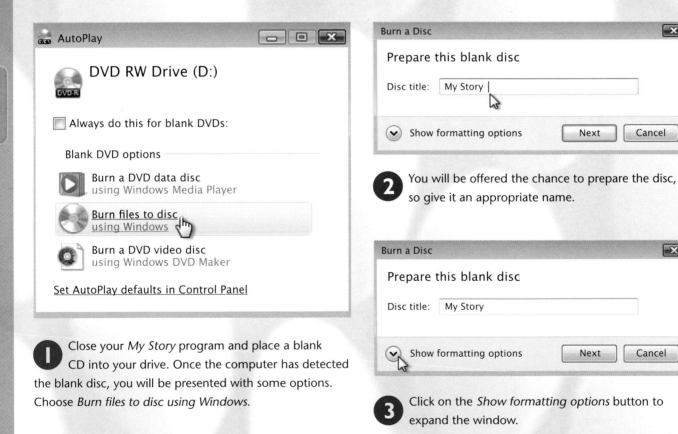

1 Close your *My Story* program and place a blank CD into your drive. Once the computer has detected the blank disc, you will be presented with some options. Choose *Burn files to disc using Windows*.

2 You will be offered the chance to prepare the disc, so give it an appropriate name.

3 Click on the *Show formatting options* button to expand the window.

Burn a Disc

Prepare this blank disc

Disc title: My Story

○ **Live File System** – Allows you to add and erase files, like a USB flash drive. Might not be readable on operating systems before Windows XP.

  <u>Change version</u>

◉ **Mastered** – Readable on all computers and some CD/DVD players. Requires you to write all files at once, and individual files can't be erased afterwards.

<u>Which CD or DVD format should I choose?</u>

⌄ Hide formatting options   [Next]   [Cancel]

4 Choose the *Mastered* option,which allows the disc you burn to work as reliably as possible.

Burn a Disc

Please wait...

Writing the data files to the disc...

[Next]   [Cancel]

6 Finally, click the *Burn to Disc* button in the "Burn" folder. This allows you to review your title and the speed at which the disc will be burned, before beginning the process with the *Next* button.

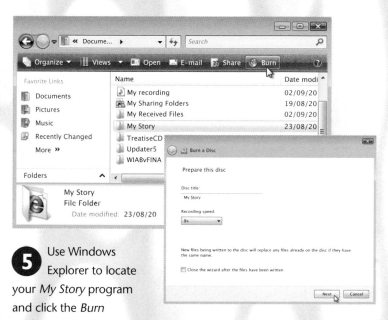

5 Use Windows Explorer to locate your *My Story* program and click the *Burn* option in the Toolbar. If you have included Movies or Audio in your project, you must also include the *My Story* folder from your computer's main hard disk (see page 48 or 51).

HELP DESK ▶

It is also possible to burn a CD on an Apple Macintosh computer. When you insert a blank disc, a "Burn Folder" is created. Open this like any other Finder window and drag the *My Story* file into it. Afterward, simply click the *Burn* button at the top right of the "Burn Folder."

Burn Folder

Creating a DVD

Although there is little difference between a DVD and CD as far as a computer is concerned—the former simply has more storage space—a DVD does have another trick up its sleeve: If it is set up properly, it can act as both a computer disc and a regular DVD. Depending on the amount of multimedia content in your story, there may be enough room to include some of the original media files at full resolution, rather than the files that have been reduced in size to fit into the *My Story* window.

HELP DESK

CDs and DVDs may look the same, but the amount of information they can store varies dramatically. A CD can hold up to 700 MB (Megabytes) of data, while a DVD can store 4.7 GB (Gigabytes), which is more than six times as much. Make sure you use the right one to save your story.

To create a project like this, you'll need a DVD-creation program such as iDVD or Windows DVD Maker. Both of these programs allow you to add your photo and video files and the menu pages that link them.

1 Open your DVD-editing program and choose your menu design from the templates provided.

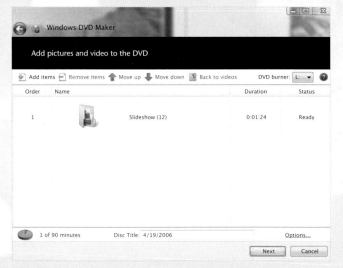

2 Add your video clips using the *Media* panel. If you choose a group of photographs, the program will offer to combine them into a slideshow—complete with transition effects—and allow you to choose and add background music.

3 Next, click *Advanced>Data Content* and drag your *My Story* application to the window. Remember that the *My Story* program should not be in use during this process.

4 If you have additional digital files you'd like to include, press the *New* button before locating and adding these files. You can add full-quality originals or files from other programs.

5 Finally, give the DVD a name and preview it on your screen before placing a blank disc into your computer and choosing *Burn*. This may take some time.

iDVD

If you are using iDVD to create your disc, add your *My Story* application via the *Advanced> Data Content* option and drag your *My Story* application to the iDVD window.

Choosing a printer

I f you don't already have a printer, there is a bewildering array of options on the market. Choosing the one that is right for you depends on three major factors: how much you will use it, whether you want to make photographic prints, and what size they will be. In addition, you may want a multifunctional device, which can act as a scanner, photocopier, and sometimes a fax machine, if you need it.

Although all printers are capable of printing photographs, some are better than others. Most printers use a mix of the printer's primary colors: cyan, magenta, yellow, and "key" (black). For better quality photo prints, some printers use additional inks to mix a greater range of colors in the same space on the page. The result is smoother color gradations.

PAPERS

Photo printers are only as good as the paper you use. Ordinary office paper, while perfectly good for letters and other documents, is not well suited for photos because the ink is drawn into the paper and tends to spread a little. Photo paper, however, is coated with a high-resolution material so the ink can mix and dry on the surface. The result is just like a traditional print from the photo shop.

Multifunctional printer
This printer has a lid that opens up as a scanner, as well as a full-color ink-jet printer. The front door opens up to reveal the paper path.

Photo printer

A wide-format photo printer can print on pages more than 12 inches (30 cm) wide at photo quality.

Access cover

To replace an empty ink cartridge, open the access door. The printer detects that the door is open and stops printing.

Input

The paper travels from the back of the printer. It can also travel along a straight path, which allows you to use thicker paper and light card stock.

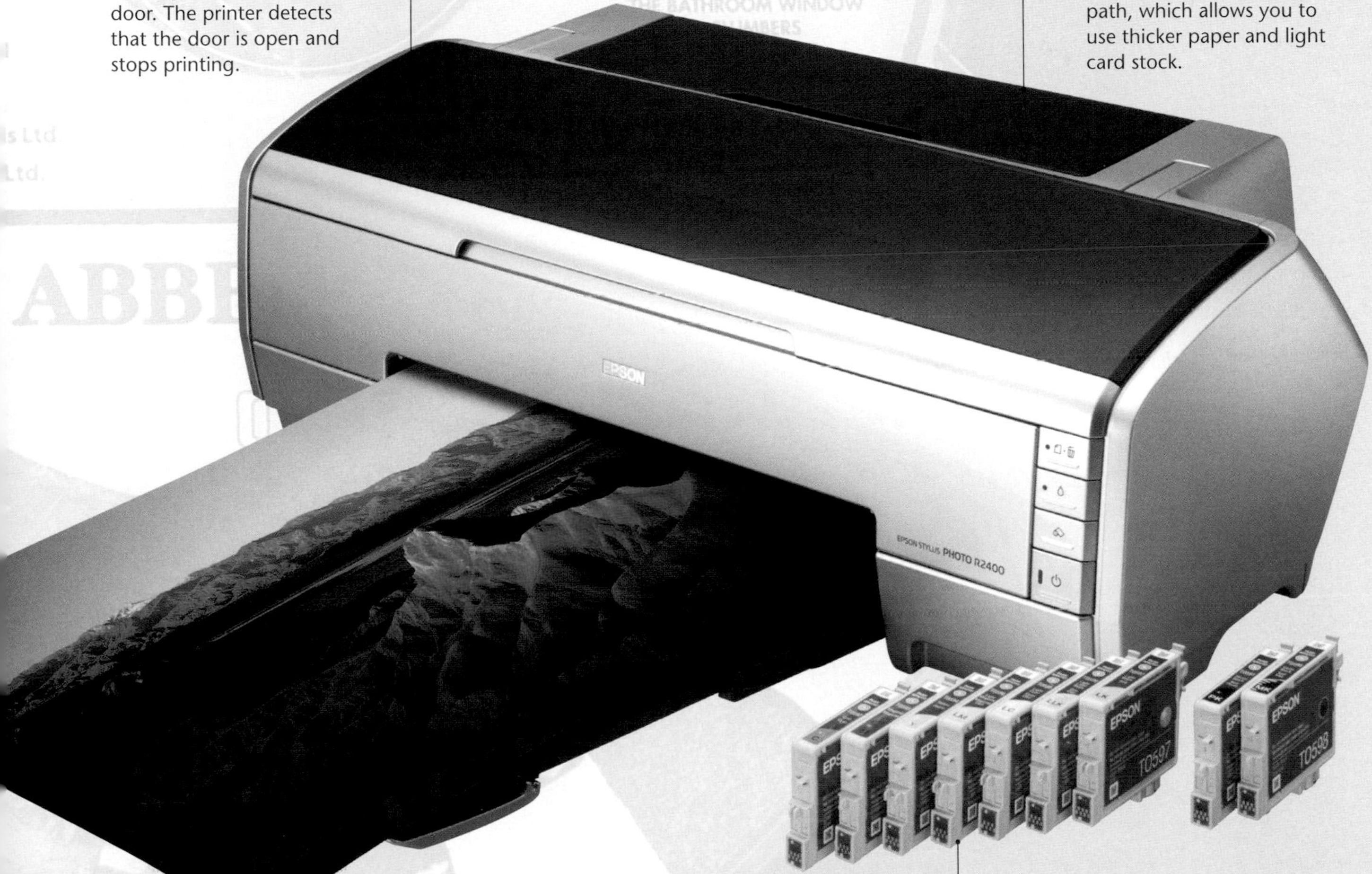

Output tray

This tray folds away so the printer will take up less space when it's not in use.

Inks

The amount of ink cartidges a printer uses depends on its make and model. In this case, nine shades—and an additional pigment, black—combine to make very smooth prints with a wide color range.

Page setup

Before you print any document, you need to check your printer settings by using the *Page Setup* tool. The tool tells the program which size paper to use and it tells the printer the orientation of the final image. Click *File>Page Setup* in the application you're using, whether it's *My Story* or Photoshop Elements.

Printers can vary in characteristics, such as how close to the edge of a page they can print. You will get the best results from your printer if your page setup is correct. It is important to take the following steps before printing. Keep in mind that when you finish, a document will not print—this is simply a preparation stage. Turn to page 108 to learn more about printing your document.

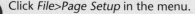

Click *File>Page Setup* in the menu.

Select the paper size you have loaded in your printer.

Page Setup

Paper

Size: Letter

Source: Automatically Select

Orientation
○ Portrait
◉ Landscape

Margins (milimeters)
Left: 0   Right: 0
Top: 0   Bottom: 0

OK   Cancel

3 If it is appropriate, you'll be asked to choose the source. Some printers have more than one tray to keep different types or sizes of pages—the source refers to the tray the printer will use.

4 If you want to print a page in landscape—if your page layout is horizontal—choose this option. You do not need to rotate the paper in the printer—the computer will print sideways.

5 Click *OK* to save these settings. They can be changed at any time by starting again at step 1.

MACINTOSH PAGE SETUP

The *Page Setup* box on a Macintosh looks slightly different than on a PC, but it essentially works the same way. Leave the first *Settings* option untouched. Note that the *Portrait* and *Landscape* options are shown as graphic buttons rather than words.

Page Setup

Settings: Page Attributes

Format for: iP5000

Paper Size: US Letter
21.59 cm x 27.94 cm

Orientation:

Scale: 100%

?   Cancel   OK

Printing a page

You can print any page you like from the database by using a home or office printer. Thanks to the high resolution of modern desktop printers, you will see all of the details on your printed page that you view on the computer screen. That means you can enjoy reading your entries even when the computer is switched off.

The printing option in *My Story* is intelligent; when you print from a list view—like the list of books in this example—your computer will automatically include all of the records, even if they do not fit onto your computer screen. When you print from a single record view, such as a page with a large picture and caption, then only the displayed page will print.

HELP DESK

All printers vary, so make sure that you have checked the manufacturer's instructions before printing.

1 After performing the *Page Setup* (see page 106), click *File>Print* in the top Menu bar.

Top-left print dialog:

Printer: iP5000
Presets: Standard
Copies & Pages
Copies: 1 ☑ Collated
Pages: ● All
○ From: 1 to: 1
? PDF▼ Preview   Cancel Print

Top-right print dialog:

Printer: iP5000
Presets: Standard
Quality & Media
Media Type: Plain Paper
Paper Source: Paper Feed Switch
Paper Allocation
Print Mode: ● Printing a top-quality photo
○ Printing tables and charts
○ Printing a composite document
○ Detailed Setting
☐ Grayscale Printing
? PDF▼ Preview   Cancel Print

2 The *Print* dialog box will appear on your computer screen. Before you click OK, make sure the printer settings are correct.

3 Most printers will require you to change the settings depending on whether you are printing a photograph or just text. Choose the *Quality and Media* or *Paper Type* option and select the option you feel is appropriate.

Bottom-left print dialog (Media Type menu open):

Printer: iP5000
Presets: Standard
Quality & Media
Media Type:
✓ Plain Paper
Photo Paper Pro
Photo Paper Plus Glossy
Photo Paper Plus Double Sided
Matte Photo Paper
Glossy Photo Paper
Hight Resolution Paper
Printable disc (recommended)
Printable disc (others)
T-Shirt Transfers
Transparencies
Envelope
Other Photo Paper

4 Most printers can print on a variety of papers, but they can achieve better results on specially coated paper. Tell your printer what kind of paper you are using via the *Media Type* option.

5 Finally, click the *Print* button and wait for the page(s) to print. If you are using an ink-jet printer, give the pages a few moments to dry before handling them.

My Favorite Books (spreadsheet screenshot)

Title	Author First Name	Author Last Name	Publisher	Pub.	Rating
1984	George	Orwell	Penguin	1948	
Pride and Prejudice	Jane	Austen	Penguin	1813	
I Know Why the Caged Bird Sings	Maya	Angelou	Bantam	1969	
To Kill a Mocking Bird	Harper	Lee	Harper Collins	1960	
Frankenstein	Mary	Shelley	Lackington, Hughes	1818	
Casino Royale	Ian	Flemming	Jonathan Cape	1953	
Of Mice and Men	John	Steinbeck	Spangler	1937	
The Grapes of Wrath	John	Steinbeck	Viking Press	1939	
Do Androids Dream of Electric Sheep	Philip K.	Dick	Doubleday	1968	
Adventures of Huckleberry Finn	Mark	Twain	Webster	1884	
Catcher in the Rye	J.D.	Salinger	Little, Brown & Co	1951	
Trainspotting	Irvine	Welsh	Penguin	1993	
Naked Lunch	William	Burroughs		1959	
Money	Martin	Amis		1984	
The Lord of the Rings	J.R.R	Tolkien		1954	
Gravity's Rainbow	Thomas	Pynchon		1973	
The Dice Man	Luke	Rienhart	Harper Collins	1971	
Atonement	Ian	McEwan		2002	
Good Omens	Terry	Pratchett	Gollancz	1990	
The Hitchhikers Guide to the Galaxy	Douglas	Adams	Pan	1979	
Dirk Gently's Holistic Detective Agency	Douglas	Adams	Pocket Books	1987	
The Butter Battle Book	Dr	Seuss	Random House	1984	
Brave New World	Aldus	Huxley	Chatto and Windus	1932	
One Flew Over the Cuckoo's Nest	Ken	Kesey	Viking	1962	
The Great Gatsby	F Scott	Fitzgerald	Charles Scribner's	1925	
On The Road	Jack	Kerouac	Viking	1957	
Odyssey	Homer			702	
Macbeth	William	Shakespeare		1623	
A Study in Scarlet	Arthur Conan	Doyle	Ward, Lock, & Co	1887	
Dream of the Red Chamber	Honglu	Meng		1700	
Silas Marner	George	Eliot	William Blackwood	1861	

MY MUSIC   MY SPORTS   MY PETS   MY HISTORICAL IDEA
MY BOOKS   MY PEOPLE   MY MEMENTOS   MY TIME OF THE YEAR
MY FILMS   MY PLACES   MY FOOD AND DRINK   MY THINGS

Blogging from *My Story*

Writing doesn't always flow easily, and a project such as *My Story* asks you to put your heart and soul onto the page. So why not reuse the material in your personal blog? You are, after all, the copyright holder of anything you write!

Many of us, of all ages, write blogs. You don't need any technical knowledge and, even you if you're not aspiring to world fame, it's a great way to communicate with family members across the globe. Of course, if you are aspiring to be famous, it seems as though building a readership on the Internet is an important step toward getting a publishing deal these days.

mystory

Monday, September 10, 2007

Still writing My Story

Writing the MyStory book has been an exciting project, giving me the chance to explore all the possibilites of the home computer.

Posted by Adam Juniper at **2:41 PM** 🖉   **0 comments**

Subscribe to: **Posts (Atom)**

① Using your Web browser, open your blog at the page you want to copy from and click and drag with your mouse to highlight the text you want to copy. Press Ctrl+C (or Apple+C) to copy the text to the computer's virtual clipboard.

② Switch to the page in *My Story* where you will paste the new text.

③ Click on the field that will receive the new text and press Ctrl+V (or Apple+V) to paste it in place. You can add type to other fields, too.

BEGINNING TO BLOG

If you've ever wanted to start blogging, there are some Web sites that will help you get going without any technical knowledge. These sites will create a page for you and allow you to log in and add a new entry whenever you please. The entries will be organized for you, and you will be given a Web address that you can share with the world.

Manage **Your Blogs**   Create a Blog | Help

You are not a member of any blogs. Create one now to start posting!

CREATE YOUR BLOG NOW

Are you looking for a blog that you think should be here?
See "My blog disappeared from my account!"

1. Choose a Web site such as www.blogger.com, run by Google, which allows you to create your own blog automatically.

2. Simply choose the name you want and check to see if it is already in use.

Name your blog

	❓	My Story		Enter a title for your blog.
Blog address (URL)	❓	http:// mystoryblog .blogspot.com		You and others will use this to read and link to your blog.
		Check Availability		
OR				
Advanced Setup		Want to host your blog somewhere else? Try Advanced Blog Setup. This will allow you to host your blog somewhere other than Blogspot.		

CONTINUE →

3. Next pick your style, perhaps using one of the examples shown at the bottom of this page.

Title: Still writing My Story

Preview

Writing the MyStory book has been an exciting project, giving me the chance to explore all the possibilities of the home computer.

4. Now you're ready to start typing an entry.

Blog design examples

Showing slides on a TV

Most modern televisions over a certain size include a socket that allows you to connect directly to your computer or indirectly via a High-Definition Multimedia Interface (HDMI) connector, which is the standard connector for High-Definition televisions.

This capability isn't available on every television or computer, but it's well worth using if you have it. If you have a laptop, you will almost certainly have an external monitor socket. All you need is a cable to connect the socket on the computer to the one on the TV. Next you can plug your laptop in whenever you like, tune the television to the computer, and use the TV display.

Some computers allow you to switch between mirroring the display you see on your small monitor onto the big screen and a dual-display mode that treats the second display as an extension of the first. Mirroring is easier to use if the displays are not next to each other, because you can use your display to make sure things are going well.

Component
This is an older standard for connecting analog High-Definition consumer electronics. It is still commonly found on HDTVs.

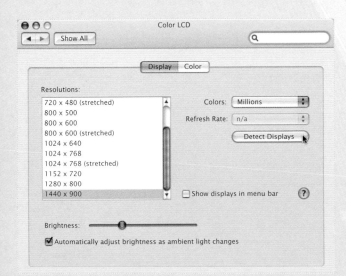

1 Check the connections on both of your devices and get a cable to link them. Remember to note whether the connector on each is female (has holes) or male (has pins) before you go to the store. You can use the table on page 113 to choose a conversion cable.

2 Switch the television to display the appropriate input. HDMI may be labeled Blu-Ray or HDTV, while VGA or DVI connections are often called PC—even if you're using a Mac.

3 If your computer doesn't automatically detect the new monitor, open the *Control Panel* or *System Preferences* display and choose *Detect Displays*.

VGA connector
Until recently this was the most common connection between a computer and monitor. It has been supplanted by the DVI connection.

DVI connector
This has become the standard for computer-to-monitor connections. It is capable of handling a newer digital or older (VGA) analog signal. Although the socket is identical, you can only use a DVI-to-HDMI cable if the computer output is digital.

HDMI connector
This is the standard digital connection for all High-Definition consumer electronics, including HDTV cable boxes, Blu-Ray players, and modern game systems.

CONVERSION CABLES

	VGA	DVI	HDMI	Component
VGA	●	●	○	○
DVI	●	●	●	●
HDMI	○	○	●	○
Component	●	●	○	●

● Link cable available   ○ No link cable available

5

Working with source material

The great thing about a completely digital project like *My Story* is that all of the files are on your computer, making it easy to edit and enhance them. That's the focus of this chapter, which introduces digital-image editing, movie making, and even how to clean up your audio files.

All of the projects in this chapter are simply ideas—there is no requirement to make any changes to your digital files. However, you might find that your memories are best served by cleaning them up a little. For example, simply trimming wasted space from around a photograph will make the part or person that is most important to you appear stronger.

Editing photos

Perhaps the biggest advantage of digital photography over film-based photography is the ability to manipulate images easily. There's no implication of impropriety here, since there are a number of reasons why altering an image can improve it—without eliminating individuals or distorting history. Of course you can do those things, too, but whether you're accurately reflecting your own story is a judgment call.

In this chapter we'll concentrate on simple techniques that can make a picture easier on the eye. These steps can be re-created in the same way in most image-editing software, but unless otherwise stated these examples use Adobe Photoshop Elements. Before proceeding to the examples, here are a few alternatives, as well as the basics of Photoshop Elements.

Windows Photo Gallery or iPhoto
You've already seen that both Macs and some Windows computers include photo-management utilities that can also help you fix your photos. While they're not as flexible as Photoshop Elements, you might find they're all you

need. So, if you don't have another program, why not start with one of these first before deciding if you want to take your editing to the next level?

Picnik and others
The brave new world of Internet editing is here, which means that you may never need a separate image-editing program. In this case, an editing program runs within your Internet browser, although these programs currently offer little more than iPhoto or Photo Gallery. They have huge potential though, and you can learn more at www.pixer.us, www.picnik.com, and www.cellsea.com.

HELP DESK

Adobe Photoshop Elements offers a simplified *Quick Fix* mode that makes it easy to make automated changes to the overall color and contrast.

Toolbar
When you are editing a photo, only one tool can be selected at a time. The selected tool—which is highlighted—affects the behavior of the mouse, so that it acts as a brush, eraser, or magnifying glass.

Tool Options bar
Because each tool can have different characteristics, the *Tool Options* bar changes to display the options for the selected tool.

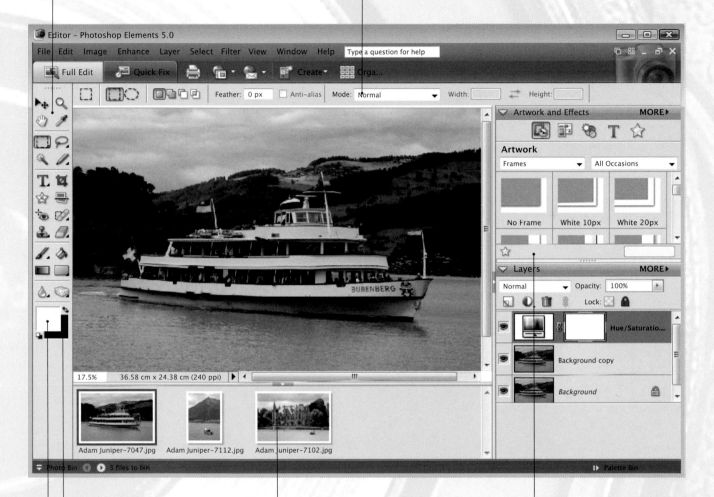

Background color

Foreground color
This is the color you will paint with if you use the *Brush* tool. If you want to change it, just click on the colored square to open the color picker.

Photo Bin
Photoshop Elements allows you to have more than one file open at a time, which is useful if you want to copy elements from one to another. All of the open files are visible in this section.

Palettes
Additional features can be contained in separate windows, which are conveniently docked against the side of the screen or switched off when they are not needed.

Cropping and rotating

If you've ever put together a photo album, you'll know that it often helps to get the scissors out and cut a picture down to size, especially if you want to eliminate any unnecessary objects near the edges of the frame.

Digital cropping provides the same possibilities, with the advantage that you won't end up with imperfect scissor lines at the edges, or a final image that is too small. In addition, if you haven't managed to hold the camera straight, you can digitally rotate the image to get a perfectly level horizon.

1 To correct a flawed horizon, click on the *Straighten* tool in the *Toolbar*. Move the cursor to a point on the horizon and click the mouse button, but do not release it.

2 With the button held down, drag the mouse to another point further along the horizon that should be level with it. Now release the button.

3 The *Straighten* tool will automatically rotate the photograph, expanding the area and adding extra space where it is necessary. These excess areas need to be removed by cropping the image.

HELP DESK

In Photoshop Elements you can rotate an image as you crop by clicking and dragging anywhere outside the crop area. The cursor will turn into a double-ended arrow. The *Straighten* tool is more accurate, but if you use the *Crop* tool you don't need to switch between tools.

iPHOTO

To crop a photo in iPhoto, select the image by scrolling to it in the *Library* and clicking on it once to highlight it. Now click the *Edit* button in the

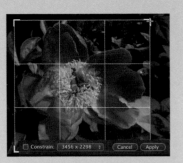

lower *Toolbar* and select the *Crop* tool. You will be able to drag the lines bounding the photo to create a new crop.

 4 Select the *Crop* tool from the *Toolbar*. Next go to the *Tool Options* bar to choose your preferred *Aspect Ratio* for the final image. If you leave this blank, your crop can take any rectangular shape you choose, but 4 x 6 inches will match most photos.

5 Now click and drag across the image area to highlight the area you want to keep. The area to be cropped is darkened.

6 You can click and drag any of the side or corner points to alter the crop. You can also click inside the crop area and drag it to another position on the page.

7 When you are ready to commit your crop, click the green *Check Mark* icon in the lower right of the crop box.

Correcting exposure

Whether you, or your camera's automatic functions, have missed the mark when it comes to the perfect settings, the most likely outcome is an image that is either too light (overexposed) or too dark (underexposed).

For example, the snowy mountain below has fooled the camera's automatic exposure settings because there is more white than it expects in an average scene. It has compensated by making things a bit too dark.

HELP DESK

Remember that you can use these techniques on any digital file—not just pictures from a digital camera. You can scan old photographs (see page 22) and fix them, too.

Auto Smart Fix

Although automatic camera settings caused the initial problem, it is likely that the computer will do a better job of fixing the photo than your camera. To try it out, click *Enhance>Auto Smart Fix*. If you don't like the result, click *Edit>Undo* to go back just as it was before. You can then try one of the alternative, manual methods.

Brightness and Contrast

If you've ever had trouble with the picture on your television, you're already familiar with the *Brightness/Contrast* control:

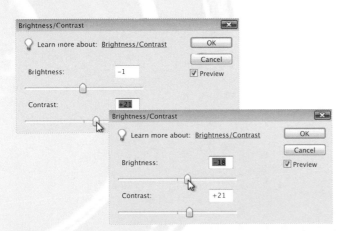

Levels

The *Levels* setting provides you with a graph, or histogram, that helps you diagnose the problems in your photo. This histogram shows how much of the image is dark, how much is light, and every value between. In this case, there are no values shown at the right end of the histogram, which means there is no pure white in the image. The largest peak, near the midpoint, represents the large area of similar tone in the image. This peak needs to move to the right, so that pure white is introduced into the picture.

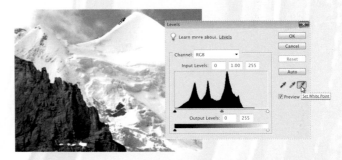

1 Click *Enhance>Adjust Lighting>Brightness/Contrast* to open the control, and make sure the *Preview* box is checked (beneath the *Cancel* button).

2 Begin by clicking and dragging the *Brightness* control to compensate for the overall darkness of the photograph.

3 Now drag the *Contrast* slider until the picture looks right. You can tweak either slider before clicking *OK*.

1 Click on the *Set White Point* dropper tool.

2 Click on an area of the image that needs to be bright white. You'll notice that the histogram immediately spreads out, right up to the highlight end. To finalize the effect, use the *Set Black Point* icon and click on an area that should be totally black.

Fixing color problems

Just as digital cameras can be fooled by light, they can also be confused by color temperature. Without delving too far into the science, the problem is that different kinds of light—such as sunlight, fluorescent tubes, or tungsten lightbulbs—give off light of different colors. When you look at something, your brain automatically compensates. This is not as easy for a camera since it cannot recognize color the way we do, because it does not understand what it is being pointed at.

HELP DESK

If there are any areas in your image that definitely need to be white, black, or any shade of gray, you can use these to set the tone for the overall image.

There are two solutions to this problem. The first is Automatic White Balance (AWB), a feature included in nearly every digital camera. This measures the light and attempts to give the correct color when you shoot. The second method is to use your computer to automatically, or manually, set the white balance.

Mixed light
In a scene with mixed light sources, it is impossible to compensate for each one. You might find that, from an artistic standpoint, it is better not to edit the image.

Enhance	Layer	Select	Filter	View	Window	Help	Type a question for help

Auto Smart Fix   Alt+Ctrl+M
Auto Levels   Shift+Ctrl+L
Auto Contrast   Alt+Shift+Ctrl+L
Auto Color Correction   Shift+Ctrl+B
Auto Sharpen
Auto Red Eye Fix   Ctrl+R

Adjust Smart Fix....   Shift+Ctrl+M
Adjust Lighting   ▶
Adjust Color   ▶   Remove Color Cast...
Convert to Black and White... Alt+Ctrl+B   Adjust Hue/Saturation...   Ctrl+U
                                    Remove Color   Shift+Ctrl+U
Unsharp Mask...   Replace Color...
Adjust Sharpness...   Adjust Color Curves...
                                    Adjust Color for Skin Tone...
                                    Defringe Layer...
                                    Color Variations...

Remove Color Cast

Learn more about: Color Cast

To Correct a Color Cast

To correct a color cast, click on a part of the image that should be either gray, white or black. Elements will adjust the photo based on where you click.

OK
Cancel
Reset
☑ Preview

① In Photoshop Elements, open the picture and click *Enhance>Adjust Color>Remove Color Cast*.

② The cursor will change to the *Eyedropper* tool. Click on the area that needs to have the color cast removed and the image will update instantly. If you are not happy with the change, try clicking on another area. Keep using the eyedropper until it looks right and then click *OK*.

Eliminating red-eye

The effect of glowing red eyes in flash photos—or red-eye—is not caused by a lack of sleep, but by light bouncing from the subject's pupils. The problem comes from increasingly compact cameras; the flash is so close to the lens that the reflection is more direct.

There are a number of ways to minimize the red-eye effect when shooting. You can provide more light though a series of pre-flashes—which cause the iris to contract—or perform a digital check for the symptoms of red-eye and automatically correct them. However, if you've taken these steps and there is still a problem, Photoshop Elements can come to the rescue.

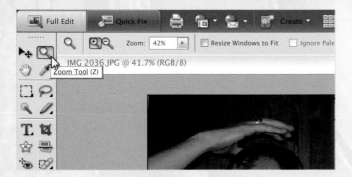

1 Open the affected image in Photoshop Elements and select the *Zoom* tool.

2 Draw a rectangle around the eyes by clicking and dragging over them. Release the mouse button when the rectangle surrounds the red eyes.

Pet eye
Animals also have reflective eyes, but the glow might not always be red. That's because they have a special light-reflecting layer behind their retinas that changes the reflected color.

③ The screen automatically zooms in on the highlighted area. Now switch to the *Red-Eye Reduction* tool in the *Toolbar*.

④ Click on each problem eye. If you need to zoom out to select another area, choose the *Zoom* tool again and click the *Fit Screen* button in the *Tool Options* bar.

iPHOTO

iPhoto, Apple's photo tool, also has the ability to automatically fix red eyes:

1. Using one of the *Catalog* views, highlight the problem image and choose the *Edit* mode.

2. To help you see what you're doing, close in on the eyes with the *Zoom* tool at the bottom-right side of the window, then select the *Red-Eye Reduction* tool from the *Toolbar*.

3. Click once on each affected pupil and it will automatically be colored black.

Converting to black & white

When photographers were limited to shooting on black-and-white film, many tricks were developed for enriching certain areas of an image. These techniques included using colored filters or the painstaking process of dodging and burning when printing images by hand.

In the digital age, it's possible to simply set your camera to a monochrome mode if you want to take black-and-white pictures. However, you can be more creative by starting with a color image. With this approach you'll always have the color version, and you can apply a variety of black-and-white effects whenever you wish. These effects balance the response to different light in much the same way as film does with colored filters.

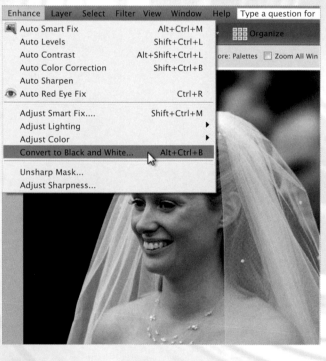

1 Open the photograph in Photoshop Elements and choose *Enhance>Convert to Black and White*.

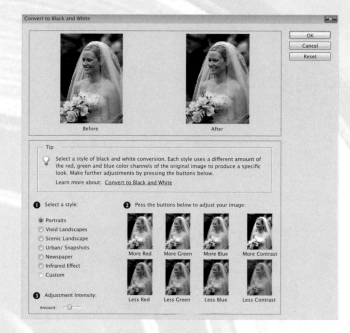

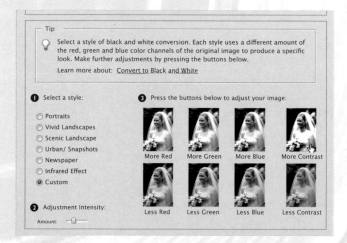

Infrared effect

A classic photographer's trick is to use infrared film to shoot landscapes. This film is especially sensitive to the light reflected from the chlorophyll in plants, but it is not so sensitive to the sky. Digital cameras cannot shoot infrared, at least not with the standard color sensors, but Photoshop Elements' black-and-white converter can simulate the effect—it looks great on landscapes!

2 Click on the style of photo that you're converting. The program will automatically make a conversion based on a preset that usually works well.

3 You can lighten or darken certain tones by clicking on one of the images in the lower-right section of the box. The "More Red" image will not make the image red, for example, but it will brighten the areas that were red in the color version.

Sharpening for *My Story*

There are many Hollywood movies in which the police (or an undercover enforcement agency) are able to take a tiny portion of a blurry photograph and somehow make a 100 percent identification of their target. This miraculous technology is, of course, impossible.

What can be done successfully, however, is to compensate for the effect of scaling photos by increasing the contrast at a local level (between the individual pixels that make up the image). This works best when you know the viewing size of the image. Here's how you can sharpen your photos:

1 Open your picture in Photoshop Elements and select the *Zoom* tool. Click *Actual Pixels*, which displays your picture so that one pixel of the image fills one pixel of your screen. There's a good chance that the whole image will not fit on the screen.

2 Now click *Image>Resize>Image Size* to bring up the *Image Resize* box. This makes it possible to alter the size of the image so that the pixels will match the space in *My Story*.

3 This box presents many choices. Make sure that *Resample Image* (at the bottom) is checked, then set the measurements to pixels using the drop-down menus in the *Pixel Dimensions* section. Set the width to 614 pixels or height to 409 and click *OK*.

4 The image is scaled to the new size. Because you are still in *Actual Pixels* (or 100 percent) zoom, this will change what you can see on the screen.

5 Click *Enhance>Adjust Sharpness* to bring up a special dialog box, and set the *Radius* to 1 pixel, then adjust the *Amount* slider to a level that looks sharp on screen. This works best if the zoom is at 100 percent. Use the +/- buttons below the *Preview* window to zoom in and out.

6 Next see if the image looks better with the *More Refined* option checked. Click OK and save the image under a new name (use *File>Save As…*) before importing the picture into *My Story*.

Before sharpening

After sharpening

HELP DESK

The optimum size for pictures in *My Story* is 409 x 614 pixels. Make sure the *Constrain Proportions* box is checked in the *Image Size* dialog. If you have a portrait-format picture, type 409 pixels into the height dialog, and the image's width will be calculated automatically. If you have a panoramic image, type 614 pixels into the width, and the height will be calculated automatically.

Adding background blur

When you're taking a photograph, it's natural to concentrate on the subject and forget about the background. That's fine, but sometimes your eyes are led away from the main subject of a picture because of sharp and distracting details in the background, which are caused by a long depth of field.

It is possible to avoid this effect when you take a picture by setting a wide aperture (represented by a low *f*-stop number). If you're lucky enough to have a camera with an aperture priority mode, your camera can do this for you. But what if you have a photo taken without these settings? Thankfully it's still possible to selectively reduce the sharp areas with the help of your computer.

1 Be sure that you can see the *Layers* palette. If not, click *Windows>Layers*. This miniature window, which might appear as a side panel of other windows, allows you to create duplicate copies of your photo. Some areas of these copies may be fully or partially transparent—in much the same way that cartoons are drawn on clear plastic cels.

2 You will see the *Background* layer in the *Layers* palette when you start editing. Click on it and drag it to the small *Create New Layer* icon in the *Layers* toolbar above it.

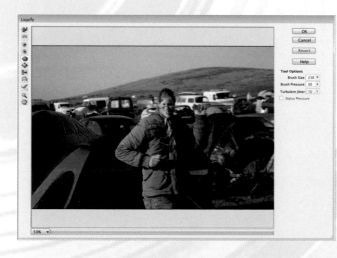

3 A new layer called *Background copy* will appear. Now that you're using more than one layer, be sure to keep track of which layer is selected as you edit. Your change will only affect the highlighted layer. Next select the original *Background* layer.

4 Click *Filter>Distort>Liquify*, which will open the *Background* layer in a new window. Select the *Pucker* tool from the left side, and use the brush-size tools on the right to adjust the size so the brush circle is a little larger than your subject.

5 Begin to click all over your subject to "suck" them inward. While this can be a fun way to alter an image, the goal is to pull some of the background in over the subject. When a blur effect is applied to the background, it will not mix any of the foreground elements and create a halo effect.

6 Continue until your whole foreground is slightly smaller, then click OK.

7 Now, back in the main program, click on the *Background copy* layer in the *Layers* panel to choose it, then reduce the *Opacity* value. You can now see through the unaltered copy to the layer you distorted to be sure the subject is smaller. Reset the *Opacity* to 100 percent afterward.

8 Select the *Magic Selection Brush* tool from the *Toolbox*. Click and drag the mouse to paint over your subject—there is no need to be accurate. Don't paint up to the edges, but try and include all of the different color areas that make up your subject.

9 When you release the mouse, a selection will be outlined by "marching ants." However, it may cover much more of the image than you had intended. If so, select the *Indicate Background* button from the *Tool Options* bar.

10 Now paint over the background areas. You don't need to be too exact or try to cover everything, but be careful not to go over the subject. When you release the mouse, you will have an accurate selection. If necessary, you can reduce the brush size and add more detail.

12 Finally click *Filter>Blur>Gaussian Blur* to apply a strong blur effect to the background. Because of the puckering, it's possible to use a higher radius without the subject becoming blurred.

11 While it's usually easier to highlight the subject, it's the background that needs eliminating. Click *Select>Inverse* to reverse the selection, then press the Delete key. Notice that now, in the *Layers* panel, there is no background on the upper layer.

QUICK METHOD

If you don't want to create such a pronounced effect, you can duplicate the layer, highlight the subject as described in steps 8–10, and then press Delete to delete the subject in the upper layer. Next switch off the selection (*Select>Deselect*) and apply a smaller blur effect to the image. This method often works well, but it often leaves sharp pixels around the edges of the subject.

Adding soft focus

While the phrase "soft focus" might conjure images of fashion shoots, the effect is—like so many things—well within your reach in the digital age. And it's somewhat more versatile.

You can take advantage of Photoshop Elements' blending modes feature to recreate a soft-focus effect in an almost limitless number of different ways. The principle each time is the same; duplicate the original image and then apply a blur to the duplicate layer. The flexibility lies in the extent to which you make the duplicate transparent—revealing the detail beneath—and your choice of blending mode.

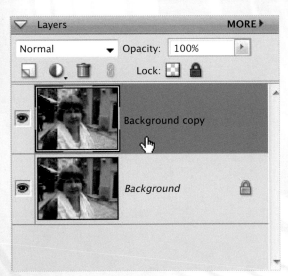

1 Open your image and duplicate the original *Background* layer by dragging it to the *Create New Layer* icon in the *Layers* panel.

2 Click *Filter>Blur>Gaussian Blur* and apply a relatively strong blur to the *Background copy* layer. Choose a level that allows you to see your subject, but eliminates all details from his or her skin and features.

3 With the upper layer still active, choose from the selection of blending modes by clicking on the *Normal* drop-down menu button. It is a good idea to experiment so you can find your favorite effect for each image. In this case, *Overlay* enhances the overall contrast.

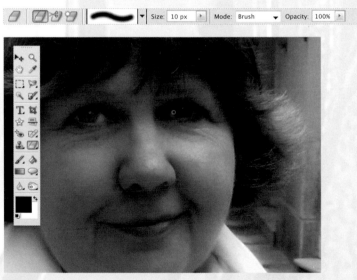

4 You can adjust the strength of the effect by reducing the *Opacity* slider next to the blending mode. This will bring back some of the original detail.

5 Finally, select the *Eraser* tool and choose a soft-edged brush from the *Tool Options* bar. Gently erase parts of the *Background copy* layer in the areas where you would like to retain full sharpness. Eyes generally benefit from this effect.

Coloring old photos

Many of us have special memories recorded in black-and-white photographs. This isn't because we didn't want to remember the colors. It's because technology didn't allow it. Perhaps the colors of these memories are vivid in your mind, and you'd like to include them in your life story.

You might not want to color all of your old photographs, because it can be time consuming. However, for very special memories, it is well worth doing. Like some of the other projects in this book, this process uses blending modes and layers to build up the original scan. There is a lot of flexibility in how you can approach this task, and the following methods will make it easy.

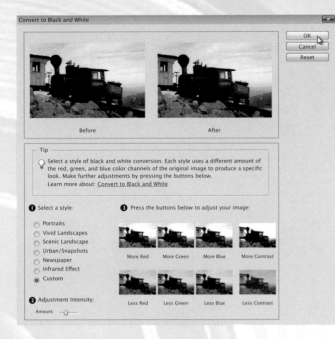

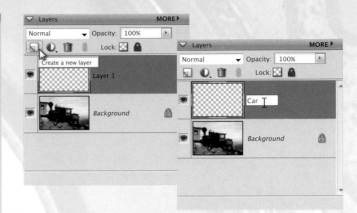

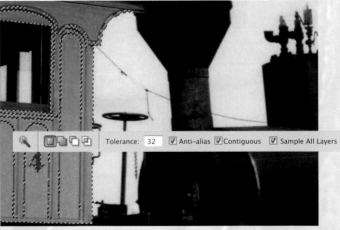

First click *Image>Enhance>Convert to Black and White* to neutralize the colors.

2 Click the *Create New Layer* icon in the *Layers* panel to create a new layer. Unlike duplicated layers, this one will be completely empty.

3 In this type of project, where you'll be creating a number of layers, it is a good idea—though not essential—to name each one. You can do this by clicking on the layer's name and typing in a new one.

4 Zoom into the area you'll be working on and select the *Magic Wand* tool. Check the *Sample All Layers* option, otherwise the program will attempt to select a region of your transparent new layer.

5 Click once inside the area you want to paint. The *Magic Wand* tool selects all of the similar colors and stops when it reaches a noticeable change in color. The number of similar colors the tool selects is adjustable via the *Tolerance* setting. Be sure *Contiguous* is checked or all similar colors across the image will be selected.

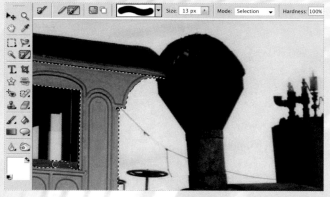

6 If the target area you want to color contains details that are outside the *Tolerance* setting, you can press Shift+click to add those areas to the selection. If that still doesn't work, choose the *Selection Brush* tool. You might need to click and hold on the *Magic Selection Brush* tool, because these tools share an icon—indicated by the marker in the lower-right corner.

7 With the *Magic Selection Brush* tool you can paint extra areas by clicking and dragging. Be careful to select an appropriate brush size from the *Tool Options* bar. Remember that holding the Shift key adds to the selection, and holding the Alt key removes areas from it.

Select	Filter	View	Window
All			Ctrl+A
Deselect			Ctrl+D
Reselect			Shift+ Ctrl+D
Inverse			Shift+Ctrl+I
All Layers			
Deselect Layers			
Similar Layers			
Feather...			Alt+Ctrl+D
Modify			▶
Grow			
Similar			
Load Selection...			
Save Selection...			
Delete Selection			

8 At this point you can choose to save the selection by clicking *Select>Save Selection*. This is useful if you change your mind about the color because you can load the selection again, using the *Load Selection* option from the same menu.

9 Click on the *Foreground Color* at the bottom of the *toolbar*. By default, this is set to black. Clicking on this button opens the color picker, which you can use to choose any color by dragging the central hue slider. When coloring images, don't add any additional black to the hue you choose.

10 Select the *Brush* tool and choose a large, soft brush size. It's also a good idea to set the *Mode* to *Normal* and the *Opacity* to 100 percent.

11 Now paint over the target area with the brush, taking care to reach every part of your selection. There is no need to worry about going over the edges—the color will stay within your selection.

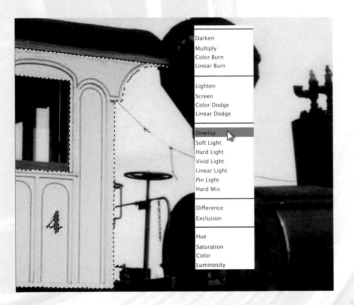

12 To restore the details, switch the blending mode for the layer. When you have a light color, *Overlay* is a good choice. However, it is worth experimenting with other blending modes for different shades, and you may use a lot of layers.

13 Before you move on to select the next area, it's necessary to click *Select>Deselect* to remove the current selection.

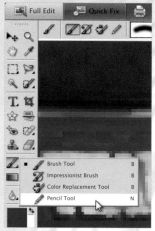

14 Continue to select and paint other areas. Remember to add a layer for each change of color and to experiment with blending modes. The *Color* mode is useful with stronger shades.

15 For some images it will be necessary to make changes at the pixel level. To do this, click and hold on select the *Brush* tool and then choose the *Pencil* tool from the menu that opens.

16 Zoom in on a problem area and click on a pixel to paint it with the selected color. Keep in mind that this won't delete the color on the layer beneath, so the stronger shade needs to be on the higher layer.

17 This image also has some linear details on the paint. The easiest way to add these is to draw them. Select the *Line* tool (one of the *Shape* tools), pick an appropriate color, and then click at the start and end of the line to draw it back in.

18 Some of the background areas need coloring, too. The mountainside behind the train doesn't have much color because it is misty, and presumably mostly rock. In this case, making a selection with a low tolerance, so that it has holes, is appropriate.

19 A color image very rarely has pure grays, so even the objects that are gray or black, such as the train and the foreground rocks, need to be lightly colored with a shade that seems natural. In this image, yellow was used for the rocks and orange was applied to the engine.

20 Finally, create an *Adjustment* layer at the top of the layer stack, to reduce the *Contrast*. This will compensate for the strong shading.

HELP DESK

Another idea is to merge your color layers in the *Layers* panel by highlighting them and pressing Ctrl+E. Although this means you will be limited in your blending mode, you can apply a small amount of *Gaussian Blur* to all the shades at once, which compensates for any imperfect selections.

If you are going to try this, it's a smart idea to duplicate your file first to keep all of the original layers safe.

Repairing photos

The great thing about memories is they are abstract—safely locked in your mind, where they can be preserved with clarity, or sometimes even tinted by rose-colored glasses.

However, photographic paper does not always stand the test of time quite as well, which is why you may need the help of photo-editing software to repair your snapshots. The photo below is an especially bad example that has been ripped in two, but these techniques would also apply to a photograph that has only been sightly torn, or to one that had simply lost a small corner. Just use the techniques that you need.

Once an image is put together, you can perform other Photoshop restorations on it, such as tweaking the color (see pages 122–123).

1 If you're dealing with a completely torn photo, scan both—or all—of the pieces together. Examine the photo closely. Often one side of the tear will need to sit above the other because one side has some visible paper that needs to be covered. Select the *Magnetic Lasso* tool.

2 Click somewhere along the broken edge and begin to move the mouse. The computer program will follow the edge as long as there is contrast between the background and the image.

3 If the program goes astray—because the contrast is lower between the image and the tear—press Delete and roll the mouse back. This will delete the previous marker point, allowing you to continue. Next time click the mouse more often to add your own control points.

4 When you reach the bottom edge of the torn section, press Alt and click on the corner.

5 Press Alt+click on the upper torn corner of the section, and add control points until you reach the next tear. The Alt+click command temporarily invokes the *Polygonal Lasso* tool, which draws straight lines between each point.

6 When you reach your starting point, click in the first square to complete the selection.

Layer	Select	Filter	View	Window	Help
New				Layer...	Shift+Ctrl+N
Duplicate Layer...				Layer From Background...	
Delete Layer					
Rename Layer...				Layer via Copy	Ctrl+J
Layer Style				Layer via Cut	Shift+Ctrl+J
New Fill Layer					
New Adjustment Layer					
Change Layer Content					
Layer Content Options					
Type					
Simplify Layer					
Group with Previous	Ctrl+G				
Ungroup	Shift+Ctrl+G				
Arrange					
Merge Layers	Ctrl+E				
Merge Visible	Shift+Ctrl+E				
Flatten Image					

7 The highlighted area can now be moved to its own layer. Press D to set the colors to default (black foreground/white background). Click *Select>New>Layer Via Cut*, which takes the selected area, replaces it with the background color, and places the selection on a new layer.

8 Switch to the *Move* tool. The new layer is now surrounded with anchor points.

9 Click inside the anchor area and drag the piece of photo so it roughly lines up with the other piece.

10 Now move the mouse just outside the highlighted area. It will turn into a curved, double-ended arrow to indicate that you can rotate the selection by clicking and dragging.

11 Make slight adjustments to the rotation and location until the two parts line up as well as possible, then click the green *Check Mark* to accept the new position.

12 Next select the *Clone Stamp* tool, which allows you to paint the texture of one area of a picture onto another. This can come in handy when touching up facial features, but in this case, the plan is to deal with some scratches and the line formed by the tear. This is also a two-step process. First you need to Alt+click on the source area—the good area you want to use as "paint."

13 Now, click and drag to paint over the damaged area. Notice that as you drag the mouse, the clone source area follows your movement at the same distance.

14 Work your way across the whole image, increasing and decreasing the size of the brush by pressing the [and] keys and by changing the sampling, or source point, as often as you need. The more you do this, the less your image will have repeated patterns.

15 If your image has torn corners, use the *Clone Stamp* tool to extend the existing detail. It's not essential that you re-create exactly what was there, as long as you give the impression that it is correct.

16 Use the Crop tool (see page 118) to set the *Aspect Ratio* to *No Restriction* and make a crop the size of your picture. Rotate it to match your picture—this is similar to step 10—before committing to the change.

17 If your image still has some minor scratches, you will want to apply a filter to correct them. But before you can, you need to flatten the layers by clicking *Layer>Flatten Image* so the filter will affect all of the layers.

18 The *Dust and Scratches* filter is useful for images that have aged badly. Set a low radius—if there are small marks—and tweak the threshold until you see most of the marks disappear without changing the image detail.

Improving a scan

When you scan a photograph, it is usually made up of even tones printed on good-quality paper. However, documents can be printed on all kinds of paper. Have you saved newspaper clippings of birth and wedding announcements or sports team successes? Newspaper is very rarely white when it is new and will only turn more yellow with age.

There are two stages to eliminating this effect. First, be sure that you use the most appropriate settings in your scanner software. Next, you'll need to compensate for the problem in your image-editing software. The first stage, scanning, is covered in steps 1 to 3. The second stage, using image editing software, is covered in steps 4 to 6. Although the later steps should look familiar if you are using Photoshop

Elements, the dialog box that appears on your screen when scanning might be different from the one shown here. Don't worry, although manufacturers vary the look and feel of their software, the functionality is similar. If you have difficulty finding the equivalent tools by their name alone, try opening any drop-down menus and reading though the options.

1 Open Photoshop Elements and locate your scanner using *File>Import*.

2 Go to your scanning program and select the highest optical resolution available on your scanner. You'll be able to find this information in your scanner's manual.

3 Choose the scanner's document or magazine mode. This will compensate better for a printed, rather than photographic, source. It is also a good idea to choose color to preserve as much image data as possible—you can eliminate it later if you change your mind.

Scan

[Scan]
Saves the scanned image and open the image by a selected program.

Scanner settings

Select source:
Scan mode:
Image quality:
Paper size:

- Black and White
- Grayscale
- ✓ Color (Magazine)
- Color (Photos)
- Color (Multi-Scan)
- Color (Auto crop)

☐ Use the scanner driver to make advanced settings

Save scanned image to

File name: Certificate 1
Save as type: TIFF

Macintosh HD:Users:a...er:Desktop:My Story: Browse...
☑ Put pictures in a subfolder using today's date

Linked scanned image to   Link Deletion

                                 Set...

Defaults   Apply   Cancel   Scan

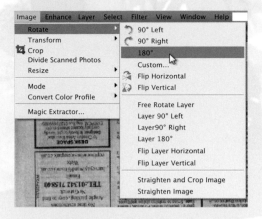

4 Click *Scan* and the document will appear in Photoshop Elements. If you placed the document the wrong way, click *Image>Rotate>180°*. Use the *Zoom* tool to view the document at 100 percent.

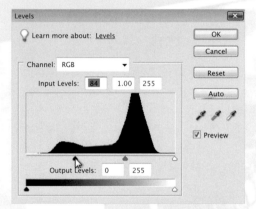

5 Open the *Levels* tool by using the menus or the *Adjustment Layers* button in the *Layers* panel. The latter allows you to make changes later without changing the original scan. Drag the black *Shadows* slider to the right until the lettering in the image appears solid black.

Color mode

6 Drag the white *Highlights* slider in until the paper is a good tone. This is an artistic decision. While you could easily make the paper all white, keeping some yellow will remind you that this is a newspaper clipping.

Grayscale mode

Black-and-White mode

Editing videos

Editing video on your computer has only recently become a practical proposition, thanks to the constant advances in computer technology and, more importantly, storage space. The latter, measured in gigabytes of hard drive space, is the crucial factor in preparing a video for *My Story* because you don't want to devote too much space to video.

HELP DESK

To create movies that are compatible with *My Story* using Windows Movie Maker you have to save them as uncompressed DV-AVI files. These take up a lot of space, so edit them to no more than five minutes.

You can make feature-length home movies if you choose, but it would be a good move to save them as DVDs. At this point, a standard computer hard drive is not big enough to store all of your videos indefinitely, so it is better to think of it as a temporary storage area while you're working on video clips.

You can create your clips with a video-editing program such as iMovie (on a Mac) or Windows Movie Maker (included with some editions of the Windows). These programs allow you to examine clips, pick out the best parts, arrange them in the order you choose, and add sounds and visual effects. After editing, you can do a number of things with the video, such as put it on the Web, make a DVD, or save it as a digital file. It's the latter step that *My Story* needs, but before you get to that stage, you'll need a movie to edit.

Windows Movie Maker

Clips
This area stores the unused clips before they are added to the project's timeline. It can also show previews of the transitions.

Tasks area
Open *Wizards* (automated step-by-step instructions) to help you through the stages of editing and importing a video.

Preview window
Lets you view clips or your entire project.

Timeline
This shows the clips in the order they will be played. You can drag your clips from the *Clips* area.

iMovie

Thumbnail size
Drag the slider to adjust the size of the video clip thumbnails.

Play head
As you move the pointer along a clip or the edited movie timeline, the play head follows you along. The frame beneath the play head is the one shown in the main viewer.

Viewer
This window shows the frame that your mouse is on, or it allows you to watch previews of the project.

Library
These clips are available to drag into the timeline and add to the movie. They can be imported from a digital video camera or another source, such as a DVD.

Thumbnail duration
Drag the slider to adjust the number of frames per thumbnail.

Tools
Use these tool buttons to access extra features, including special effects and sounds.

Improving video quality

Home movies can be prone to a number of problems. If you let the kids shoot them, you can guarantee there will be too much zoom and perhaps a bit too much camera shake. But it isn't just youth who fall prey to camera problems. Exposure can also be a problem, since it is something the camera generally handles.

The automated functions in modern cameras—even in older camcorders—are very good at assessing the situation at the moment the frame is shot. However, they are not so adept at comparing that moment to others.

Therefore, when you're editing clips shot sequentially, the colors can often appear completely different. The solution, known as color grading by professionals, is to adjust each clip individually in your editing program.

1 These three clips of the Statue of Liberty were all taken at roughly the same time, but as the clouds were thickening. They have been dragged into the upper movie timeline but the brightness of the clouds has affected the exposure in some of the clips.

2 Click on one of the clips you would like to fix and click on the *Adjust Video* button (or the *Effects* button if you're using Windows Movie Maker). This will bring up your options for the clip.

3 Drag the *Exposure* slider down slightly so you can see more blue in the sky between the clouds. Don't worry if the shade isn't exactly what you want, just try and be sure that the overall strength of the sky is similar to your favorite clip from the sequence.

4 The cloudy clips seem to have lost some of their blue because the camera has set a different white balance. You can restore it gradually by dragging the dot from the center of the *White Point* circle toward the blue side.

5 To restore the clip's contrast, you can either tweak the *Contrast* slider or push the markers at the ends of the *Levels* display for a more accurate enhancement.

6 Finally, repeat these steps with the other clips in the sequence. While the thumbnails will remain the same in appearance, you'll see the improvement when you preview the movie.

Composing a sequence

Editing a movie is all about leaving things out. You can shoot hours of material but still get your message across with only a few moments. For *My Story* you should aim to keep your clips to about five minutes at most—treat video clips as the highlights of your life, not every waking moment. The trick of editing a sequence is evoking the key memories, moments, and feelings from a shoot, so the first step is always to review the material.

Professional editors typically use a bin to store their clips, and this is represented in the video-editing software by the *Library* area (iMovie) or the *Media* area (Windows Movie Maker). You can use this collection to choose material to review, edit, and add to your final project. It isn't necessary to use the clips in the order they were shot, or use the same sounds. After organizing the sequence of the edit, the editor can add effects, music, and titles, but it's always best to get the order down first.

Editing in iMovie

1 Start a new project by clicking *File>New* and give it a name.

2 Is there a better way to open a sequence on New York than with a shot of the Statue of Liberty? Toward the end of the shot, however, the camera pans away from the statue, so only the first half of the shot is needed. Click and drag along the clip in the *Library* area to mark the proportion (in seconds) you want to keep, then release the mouse.

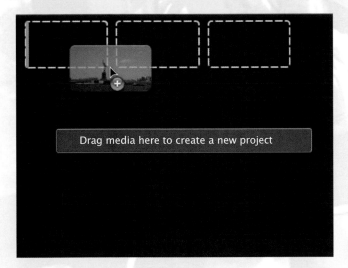

3 The yellow marker remains to indicate the selected portion of the clip. Now click and drag the clip to the *Timeline* and the highlighted portion will be part of your movie. The whole clip remains in the *Library* for later use.

4 Although it wasn't next in the shooting sequence, the shot of Battery Park seems the next logical clip to add. Click on it and press Space to preview it in the main viewer.

6 To see a little more of what is going on in each of the *Library* shots, drag the *Frames per thumbnail* slider in the bottom right of the *Library* area down to 2 seconds (2s). Now a frame is created for every 2 seconds of video in each clip, so it's easier to pick out long pans of the city.

5 It seems to be perfect as it is—with no need for trimming, so drag it straight to the *Timeline* after the Statue of Liberty shot.

7 Continue to add clips to your project. In this case, two pans from either side of the Empire State Building are added, as well as some more clips.

8 If you add a clip but still want to trim it, don't worry. Move over it just as you did when trimming clips in the *Library* area (see step 2).

9 Now hold down the Ctrl key (or right mouse button) and choose *Trim to Selection*. The clip will be shortened. In this case, it will emphasize the flag.

10 To play your sequence from the beginning, click *View>Play from Beginning* or press the Backslash (\) key. This gives you a chance to review your work in the *Preview* window.

WINDOWS MOVIE MAKER

Although there are many similarities to iMovie, this program works in a slightly different way. Rather than trimming clips by highlighting them, you need to double click on the clip in the *Media* area and set *In* and *Out* points—the start and end points for the clip.

3. To build up your project, continue adding clips by dragging them into the *Timeline*.

1. Import your video with one of the *Wizards* to the left, then choose the clip you want to add.

4. If you want to remove part of a clip, click on it and play it until you reach the frame you want. Next click the *Split Clip* button to the right.

2. Drag the clip to one of the gaps in the *Timeline*—or between two clips if you prefer.

5. The clip will split into two pieces. Drag the part you want to the *Timeline*.

Creating transitions

Sequencing your clips in order is a good start, but it can lead to some awkward changes from one clip to another. Improving the exposure of your shots (see page 150) will minimize this, but smooth transitions are a better solution.

Transitions do more than just link clips; they are part of the language of cinema and need to be treated with respect. Some effects that might seem like fun, such as a ripple effect, might be evocative of a dream sequence in the right settings. Others, like a clock wipe, have the obvious purpose of indicating the passage of time.

Some directors abhor everything but simple cuts and dissolves (fading between shots), although George Lucas made extensive use of "wipes" in *Star Wars*. In other words, using transitions is a matter of choice rather than professionalism, but try to use them appropriately.

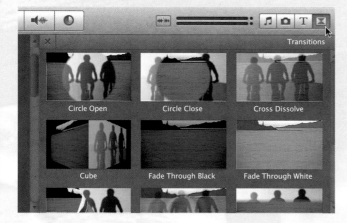

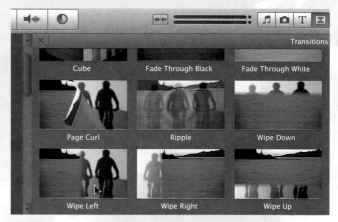

1 Click the *Transitions* button to open the *Transitions* viewer. In both iMovie and Windows Movie Maker they are presented as thumbnails, which makes it easy to see their effects.

2 Review the join between the clips that a transition is needed between—in this case, the two pans from the Empire State Building. As the camera moves right, all of the buildings travel left on the screen. Therefore, the best choice is the *Wipe Left* transition. Click and drag the *Wipe Left* transition thumbnail from the *Transitions Library* to the gap that needs the new transition.

3 You'll notice a new *Transition* icon appears in the *Timeline* between the two clips. Slide the mouse over it to preview the transition in the main viewer.

4 To have your movie start by fading up from black, choose the *Fade Through Black* transition and drag it to the gap before the first clip of the movie.

5 Review your transition (see step 3).

6 To change the duration of your transitions, right click on one of the *Transition* icons and choose *Project Properties* from the pop-up menu. Adjust the *Transition Duration* slider. All of the other transitions in the project are automatically adjusted—those on shorter clips are automatically given shorter transitions.

WINDOWS MOVIE MAKER

Just like iMovie, it's a matter of dragging your chosen transition from the *Transitions* area to the gaps between the assembled clips. To view the available transitions, choose *Transitions* from the *Tasks* list.

Adding titles

One of the joys of digital moviemaking is the ability to add professional-looking titles to your project. This doesn't mean that every frame of your movie requires captioning, but it does add a nice touch to your video project.

For a short movie, such as one for *My Story*, it's a good idea to add a title at the beginning and use captions to mark the passage of time—especially if your video represents a few days. Credits at the end are a fun reminder of who was behind the camera, too.

1 Open the *Titles Library* by clicking on the button marked "T" to the right of the central bar.

2 Choose a title style from the designs in the library and drag it to the clip you want to use.

3 In the Main Viewer, click on the text to bring up a cursor. Use the cursor keys (arrow keys) to move around the sample text and delete it, before typing in your own title for your clip.

4 If you'd like to change the size or style of the font, click on the *Fonts* button at the top left of the Main Viewer. Use the *Fonts* menu, which you may recognize from other programs, to choose the font.

1.8s – Visiting the Big Apple

0.0s from clip start – 22s total   2s

5 When you have finished editing the text, you may find that the caption space isn't long enough. If so, click on the right end of the title marker above the clip and drag to extend it.

6 To add closing credits over a black background, rather than over your clips, choose the *Scrolling Credits* title style and drag it to the gap after the final clip. You can edit your credits by clicking on the default text.

Show Fonts   **Starring** |▶| Done

Iris	as Bridgette
Tore	as Ivo
Bridgette	as Iris
Ivo	as Tore

WINDOWS MOVIE MAKER

The process for adding special effects in Windows Movie Maker is very similar to the methods in iMovie. However, you will find the library of effects in a list on the left side of the screen rather than a special icon.

7 Preview your credit clip by moving the play head to the end of the previous clip and pressing the Space bar. If the credits are too fast, you can extend them (see step 5).

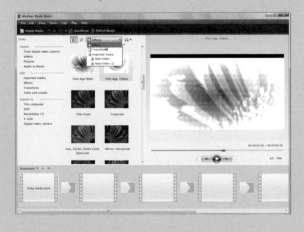

Exporting your movie

When you've completed your movie masterpiece, you'll need to export it as a computer file to *My Story*. Your video-editing software may also give you the option to create a DVD of your movie or add it to an Internet sharing site. Considering all of the work you've put into the edited movie, there is no reason you shouldn't use these. However, to import it into *My Story*, you'll need to choose the *Export* option.

This process varies from program to program, but the essentials are the same. The video-editing program must review your work and create a single new file.

This doesn't need to be the same size as your original—it is an opportunity to discard some detail in order to compress the file size.

iMovie

1 Start by choosing *Share>Export Movie* from the menu.

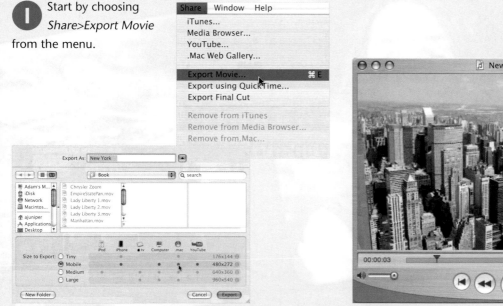

2 Choose the quality of movie you would like to save. *Mobile* or *Medium* are sensible choices for *My Story*, but both sacrifice some of the movie's detail to create a smaller file.

3 Click *Export* and wait while the computer processes your video. When it's finished, you will be able to open the video with the QuickTime player.

Windows Movie Maker

Unfortunately this program will only save video in its proprietary Windows Media format—which is not compatible with *My Story*. However, it can also save a full-size original Digital Video file, which is compatible, but the file sizes are generally large so you will need to trim your video to a reasonable length—five minutes or less is good.

1 Click *Publish to this Computer* in the list of tasks to the left.

2 Select the *DV-AVI* format and click *Publish*.

OTHER SOFTWARE

When using other editing programs, look for options that are either QuickTime compatible or recognized by all media systems including QuickTime. MPEG, MPEG2, and MP4 are good choices, as is H.264, which is an extension to MP4 that reduces file sizes but takes longer to prepare when you export the file.

The example here is Adobe Premiere Elements— often sold with Photoshop Elements. It offers a full-featured *Export* utility via the *File>Share* command. This will create digital files for *My Story*, DVDs, and High-Definition Blu-Ray discs.

Editing audio

Pages 28–35 reviewed some methods you can use to copy sound onto your computer to add it to your project. This process often involves copying, or sampling, from a less-than-perfect original source, such as an audio cassette—which is known for a considerable hiss that can be heard by most people.

Digital mastering has eliminated many sound problems like this from CDs and good-quality MP3s from stores such as iTunes. But what if you are making your own recordings?

Luckily some of the technology used by professionals when they master sound is available for your computer, too. Each program offers different abilities:

GarageBand

Included with all Apple computers, GarageBand is designed to allow you to record your own music or make your own voice-based podcasts, which are broadcast over the Internet. It also has the ability to record from the microphone or line-in socket and to export to MP3 (see page 165).

Stereo Waveform
Left and Right audio tracks are represented by separate waveforms. (For more on Waveforms, see Audacity on page 163).

Podcast material
If you're creating a podcast, GarageBand allows you to add images that appear on the screen as the podcast is viewed on Apple iPods with color screens.

Voices
GarageBand allows you to layer sounds on top of each other so, for example, you can place a jingle above a voice recording. Here only one track, Male Voice, is being used.

Jingles
A selection of pre-recorded jingles to add to your recordings by pressing the *Loop Browser* button.

Audacity

This program is being developed by an online community as an open-source project, which means anyone can view the nuts and bolts that make the program work. That means it is available for both Mac and Windows for free, and it has become a sophisticated utility, with all the features you might need. Even if you're not familiar with open-source programs, it's worth downloading it and trying it out, but choose the most recent full version, not one marked beta. A beta may have bugs that can cause the program to fail unexpectedly.

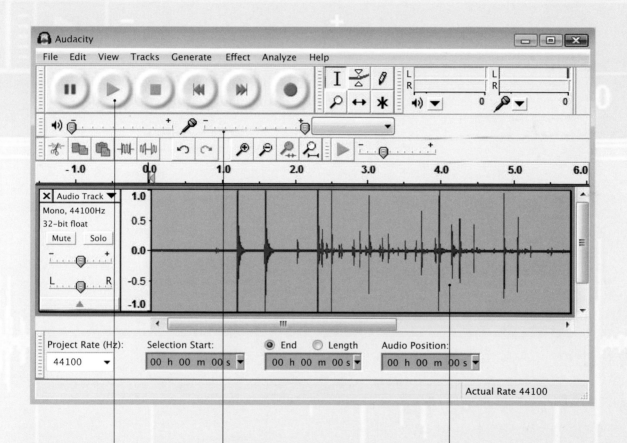

Controls
The *Play*, *Pause*, and *Record* controls will be familiar from household CD players and other audio equipment.

Input
Adjusting this volume slider controls the volume of the sound that the computer records from the microphone. If the spikes in the waveform are consistently too high (touching the edge), turn it down. If the recording is too quiet, turn it up.

Waveform
The common way to represent recorded sound on a computer is to use a waveform. The spikes extend farther from the center, the louder the sound recorded at that point.

Cleaning up an audio file

The two key elements of cleaning up any sounds that you add to *My Story* are trimming them to the right length and eliminating artifacts on the recording, such as hisses, clicks, or crackles. The proper length ensures a good listening experience as users browse your story, so you need to avoid a silent period when the user first plays the clip.

You may want to keep some crackle in a soundtrack if it represents the era, but there are few good reasons to keep tape hiss. If you are going to try to eliminate tape hiss, you'll need to do it before trimming the clip, because the computer can use the otherwise silent portion of the clip to assess and eliminate the hiss from the rest of the file.

Audacity

1 Open your audio clip in Audacity (or record directly into it using the *Record* button on the toolbar). Highlight one of the sections at the beginning of the waveform that represents the clip.

2 Choose *Effect>Noise Removal* from the menu bar to open the *Noise Removal* tool.

3 In the *Noise Removal* box, choose *Get Noise Profile*. This analyzes the section of music you have highlighted in step 1.

4 Now select the whole clip by pressing Ctrl+A in the *Soundtrack* window.

Noise Removal

Noise Removal by Dominic Mazzoni

Step 1

Select a few seconds of just noise so Audacity knows what to filter out, then click Get Noise Profile:

Get Noise Profile

Step 2

Select all of the audio you want filtered, choose how much noise you want filtered out, and the click 'OK' to remove noise.

Noise reduction (dB): 24

Frequency smoothing (Hz): 150

Attack/decay time (secs): 0.15

Preview   OK   Cancel

5 Select the *Noise Filter* (see step 2), but this time click OK at the bottom. The computer will eliminate sounds similar to those it found in the "silent" portion all the way through your audio clip.

6 Notice how the line running along the center of the clip, representing the volume in the quiet areas, is now much thinner. Now click and drag from the beginning of the clip—just before where the sound starts—to the end.

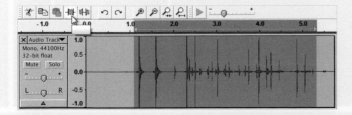

7 Click the *Trim* button. The excess silent portions on either side of your highlighted area will be deleted.

GARAGEBAND

One of the advantages of GarageBand is an automatic setting designed to get the best sound from a male or female voice. If you want to record your own voice or make a copy of an old recording of a voice, follow these steps:

Create New Music Project

Open An Existing Project

Magic GarageBand

Create New Podcast Episode

1. When you start the program, choose the *Create New Podcast Episode* option.

Podcast Track

Male Voice

Female Voice

Jingles

2. Click on either the *Male Voice* or *Female Voice* icon at the left of the screen.

3. Click on the *Record* button and start speaking into the microphone, or start the recording you want to use.

4. Click the *Play* icon again to stop. You can now use the program's other tools to trim the clip.

Converting to MP3 files

Once you've made your recording, you'll need to save it as an industry-standard MP3 file format to make the best use of space on your computer. *My Story* will accept other formats, such as Wave (.WAV), but MP3 is a logical choice because of its popularity and efficiency. It is necessary to convert to one of these formats if you started with a Windows Media file.

MP3 allows for different bit-rates, which means the amount of computer information (or bits) used for each second of the recording. This equates to the long-play option on a video recorder—the more bits used, the better the sound quality. However, you'll need more space. The best option is usually 128 Kbps. Do not go lower than 64 Kbps because you will start experiencing poor sound quality, even on computer speakers.

Audacity

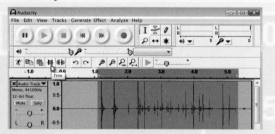

 Open Audacity and open your audio clip using the *File>Open* option.

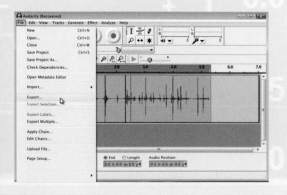

Click *File>Export*.

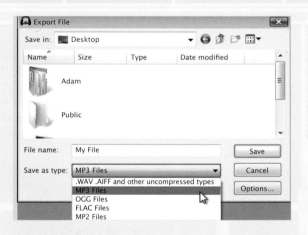

Select MP3 in the *Save As Type* field and choose a location for your file to be saved. The file will automatically be saved at the highest quality.

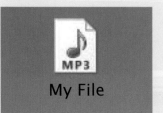

My File

An MP3 file will appear where you asked the computer to place it.

GARAGEBAND

GarageBand offers extensive export options, including the possibility of saving your recording as a podcast that can be downloaded by users across the Internet via iTunes.

With so many options it's essential to choose carefully as you export your files, especially if you want to share them as a podcast via the Internet. When you are saving sounds for the specific purpose of including them in *My Story*, be sure that they are compatible and an efficient file size. You can achieve this by taking the following steps:

1. Choose *Share>Export Podcast to Disk*.

2. Choose *Compress Using MP3 Encoder* (rather than AAC).

3. Choose *Spoken* or *Musical* podcast depending on whether you want to record at 64 Kbps or 128 Kbps. The higher quality is recommended if you've used jingles or music in your recording.

4. Click *Export* to save the file.

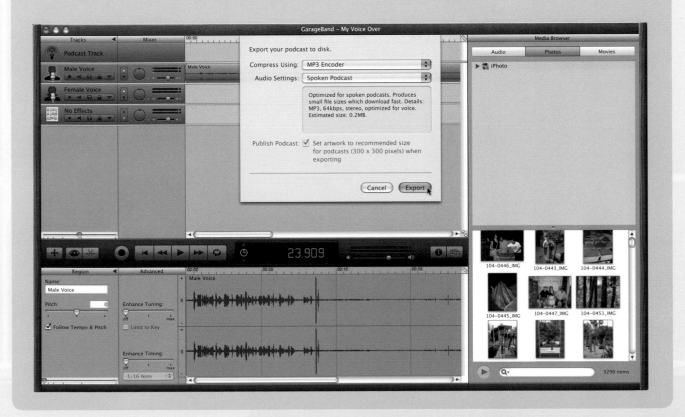

Useful resources

When you're compiling the story of your life, using a variety of digital file formats as *My Story* allows you to do, chances are you will need to call on a similarly broad variety of tools and resources to help you. Over the course of this book, and especially in Chapter Five, we have seen a lot of the software tools and learned how they can be used to perfect your media files.

There is, however, a much wider variety of tools available on the market than those used in Chapter Five, and you are not restricted to using the ones shown. Because there are established file formats, you'll find a whole host of tools that you can use. Some you might already have installed on your computer system, while others you might be able to download from the Internet or find on a magazine's cover CD. In some cases, you can even find software tools on the Internet that you can use without every having to download them. On this page we'll look at some of the programs and addresses you might find useful.

Picnik (www.picnik.com)
This is a free online image-editing tool. Simply type the address into your Web browser and click *Upload Photo*. Wait while your picture is transferred to the remote computer, then make changes using the controls. All the action takes place within your Web browser, so you'll need a broadband Internet connection to make it run quickly.

Photoshop Lightroom (www.adobe.com)
If you have invested in a Digital SLR camera you obviously take your photography seriously. If so, a program like Lightroom is almost essential. It allows you to manipulate raw files, making full use of every bit of detail your camera can record. You can then export JPEG images for inclusion in *My Story*, as well as full-size digital negatives for your archives. It is available for Windows and Mac OS X.

INTERNET SITES

www.facebook.com
Track down your old friends from school and find out what they are doing now. Exchange photos to include in your story.

www.idrive.com
This online backup service allows you to keep backups on the Internet via a broadband connection. Some space is available for free.

www.imdb.com
The Internet Movie Database works like Google, but it is tailored specifically for films.

www.readersdigest.com (www.rd.com)
Find some of your favorite music, features, recipes, provoking stories, jokes, and laughs to include in your story.

www.web-linked.com/timeus
Although all of the information in this book has been checked and edited to be as accurate as possible, computer systems develop and issues arise that cannot be forseen. For that reason, you'll find a list of Frequently Asked Questions and answers on the Internet. If you have any problems with *My Story*, make this your first port of call.

www.wikipedia.com
As well as its function as an amateur encyclopedia, Wikipedia also has many entries including "Wikipedia Commons" licensed images. You can download these to include in any *My Story* pages that need images or media files.

CONVERSION TOOLS

Sometimes you find yourself using a video or audio-editing program that cannot work with the file format that you need to produce. The best option is to find a different program, since that will avoid a whole conversion stage; however, if you can't find one, there are programs on the market with only one purpose: converting files to other more useful formats.

Any Video Converter for Windows is one such utility and is highly recommended. Visit **www.any-video-converter.com/products/for_video_free/**

VisualHub and sister program iSquint, (the latter is free) are ideal for a range of conversions for Macs. Visit **www.techspansion.com/visualhub/**

Glossary

Advanced Audio Codec (AAC)
An alternative to the popular MP3 format for audio files that can also be played by portable music devices.

Blu-Ray Disc
A new standard of computer disc for High Definition video. Blu-Ray discs are similar in appearance to CDs and DVDs, but have a much higher storage capacity. A recordable version is available.

Broadband
A collective term for different methods of high-speed Internet access. These include leased lines, cable, or DSL solutions. Broadband is recommended if you need to download large files from the Internet such as movies, or transfer images to an online lab because of its speed.

Burning
In computer terminology the verb "to burn" refers to the act of recording information to a CD, DVD, or Blu-Ray Disc (known collectively as "optical media").

Button
In computer terminology, this refers to a graphic or icon on your screen that you can "press" by clicking on it with your mouse.

Cine film
Sometimes called Ciné, the word literally means "moving." It refers to the home-movie formats that existed before video-based systems. These are 8 mm, 9.5 mm, 16 mm and Super 8.

Checkbox
In computer terminology, this refers to a box that you can click on to select a property. Usually that property will be named next to the checkbox. When the checkbox is selected, a check mark will appear in the box. Clicking on it again will deselect—or uncheck—the box.

Codec (EnCOder-DECoder)
This is the common word for the software that helps your computer unlock an audio or video file format. For example, if you want to play a video file encoded with MP4, you will need the MP4 codec installed on your computer. This is normally built in to the operating system.

CD-R and CD-RW
These are writable (CD-R) and re-writable (CD-RW) discs based on the CD format (see CD-ROM). Computers can record, or burn, data onto these discs.

Compact Disc Read Only Memory (CD-ROM)
A disc that uses the same design as an audio CD, but stores computer information and can be read only by computers.

Data
A computer term to describe any information. You might say, for example, that once you have created a new record for the name and address of one of your friends you have "added data to the name and address fields."

Digital Versatile Disc (DVD)
A high-performance disc format that was designed as the Digital Video Disc, but was adopted by computers because of its ability to hold a large amount of computer data. A DVD can store 4.7 GB (single layer) or 9 GB (dual layer).

Directory
A specially named area, or folder, stored on a computer disc. You can place files within a directory.

Exporting

Saving a file or group of files from an editing or cataloging program is known as exporting. The files can be saved in a common format that is likely to be compatible with another program, such as JPEG or TIFF for images, or MP3 for audio. For example, you might export a photo from a catalog as a JPEG file so you can import it into the *My Story* program.

Field

The individual boxes within any of the records in *My Story* that you use to add information. For example "First Name" is a field, because it only requires you to add one separate piece of information. Similarly, a long caption is just one field, too. You can tell that you are switching fields because you need to click on a new one.

Finder

The finder is the component of Mac OS X that allows users of Apple Macintosh computers to navigate through the files, folders (also known as directories), and applications stored on the computer, on inserted discs, and on any network connected to the computer.

FireWire

A common name for the IEEE 1394 or i.Link standard conection. This is a common socket on computers and digital devices, which was designed for the reliable high-speed transfer of large amounts of data, such as video, and the control of external devices. It is common on digital camcorders, which can be controlled using stop, play, and wind buttons from the computer.

i.Link

A trade name used to describe the "FireWire" or IEEE 1394 connection standard.

Importing

This is the process of moving a file into another program and—if necessary—converting it into a format compatible with that program. The term is applied when you are copying images from your digital camera to an image-cataloging program.

iMovie

A basic, but easy to use, video-editing tool that is supplied with all Apple Macintosh computers. This is an ideal program for editing short movie clips to add to your *My Story* records.

iPhoto

A photo-cataloging and image-editing program supplied with all new Apple Macintosh computers.

iTunes

A free music-cataloging program for both Apple Macintosh or Microsoft Windows computers. This is an ideal tool for keeping track of a music collection and for converting files to the MP3 format, which can be imported into *My Story*.

Joint Photographic Experts Group (JPEG)

This is the most common file format for digital images. If you have a digital camera, it will almost always save files in this format. Its popularity stems from its efficiency in compressing images to fit onto the limited storage space of digital media. It achieves this by discarding some of the details according to settings you choose when you save the file from an image-editing program, or in your camera.

Lossy compression

Compression that discards some of the detail in order to create smaller computer files. For example, lossy techniques are used by JPEG picture files and MP3 audio files.

MP3 (MPEG-1 Audio Layer 3)

Usually known by its abbreviation, MP3 files are the most common way of saving music on computers and portable players. Portable players, like Apple's iPod, are often known simply as MP3 players.

MPEG (Motion Picture Experts Group)

This is a common form of computer video file, often identified by the file extensions .mpeg or .mpg. Like JPEG, it uses a lossy compression to reduce file sizes, and subsequent versions of the standard MPEG-2 and MPEG-4 (also known as MP4) have continued to dominate computer video.

Network

A network is formed by the connection of two or more computers. Files can then be shared without having to copy them onto external discs.

Photoshop Elements

Photoshop Elements is a digital image-editing program that can be bought separately and installed on your computer. It has a variety of tools for repairing and changing your digital images. There are different versions available for both Apple Macintosh and Microsoft Windows computers. The latter also includes an image-cataloging function, while the Mac version works with iPhoto's catalog.

Pixels Per Inch (PPI)

This refers to the level of detail in a digital image file. It is especially important when you are acquiring the file (for example, scanning it). A typical scan intended to be viewed only on screen at 96 ppi means that every square inch of a picture would be represented by $96 \times 96 = 9{,}216$ pixels. 96 ppi is a good resolution for digital files. 300 ppi is better for files you will be printing, but it uses more file space.

Premier Elements

This is a digital video-editing program from Adobe—the same software manufacturer as Photoshop. It has a variety of sophisticated tools, including the ability to edit High Definition video and export to the latest Blu-Ray discs. It is also an excellent tool for editing movies and exporting them to add to *My Story*.

QuickTime

QuickTime is a common video file format on both Apple Macintosh and Windows computers. A program to play the files, called QuickTime Player, is available for free from Apple (www.apple.com). QuickTime can also play files based on open standards, such as MPEG. *My Story* uses the QuickTime system to play MPEG and QuickTime video files without leaving the *My Story* program.

Raw file

High-end digital cameras, especially Single Lens Reflex (SLR) cameras, can save Raw files. These files include all of the original information seen by the image sensor, and all of the information recorded by the camera's onboard measuring devices, but processing is not applied. Instead, the processing is handled by the computer when the file is imported. Therefore the maximum amount of information is available when images are processed on your computer. The disadvantage is that the processing stage is mandatory, and the software used must be aware of your specific camera model to interpret the Raw data.

Record

A record is a single entry in *My Story*. For example, if you add the details of a book, you create a single record composed of a Title, Author's First Name, Author's Last Name, Publisher, Year of Publication, and Rating. The individual parts of the record are called fields.

Rip
The process of converting one type of digital file—usually audio or video—to another. Ripping a video file can be a time-consuming process.

Scanner
A device for converting printed photographs, slides, or negatives into computer files.

Tagged Image File Format (TIFF)
A standard file format for saving image files that is commonly used by professionals because it does not discard any details. This is known as a "lossless" file format, but as there is no compression of the data, the file sizes can be very large.

Universal Serial Bus (USB)
The most common socket for connecting peripheral accessories to a computer. USB and USB 2.0 use the same sockets, automatically switching to the faster speed—or bandwidth— available when both the computer and USB device are USB 2.0 compatible. USB devices include printers, mice, external hard drives, scanners, and more. USB cables can even carry a certain amount of electricity, so some devices need no additional power.

USB Hub
If you don't have enough USB sockets on your computer, you can connect a hub that allows you to plug more than one device into the same socket.

World Wide Web (Web)
You can look at, or browse, pages that are stored on computers around the world by using a Web Browser. These pages, or Web sites, are the ideal place to find photographs and conduct research if you want to add detail to captions in *My Story*.

Windows Explorer
Windows Explorer is the part of Microsoft Windows that you use to navigate the files and folders stored on your computer's hard drive and any external media that you have inserted. Explorer also allows you to browse the contents of other computers via a network.

Windows Movie Maker
A basic, but easy-to-use video-editing tool that is supplied with most versions of Windows (including Windows Vista Home Premium and Windows Vista Ultimate).

Index

Acknowledgments

The author would like to thank Jules, without whose generous sacrifice and continued encouragement this book would never have been finished.

Many thanks also to all those who agreed to appear in the book, especially Lynne, Baz, Emily, Bounder, Joc, Jenny, Skye and, of course, the town of Concord, MA.

Credit is really due, however, to Alastair, Robin, and Stewart, the brains behind the *My Story* program on which all of this is based.